Safe Within These Walls

De-escalating School Situations
Before They Become Crises

Andra Medea, M.A.

Maupin House *by*
capstone
professional

Safe Within These Walls:
De-escalating School Situations Before They Become Crisis
By Andra Medea, M.A.

Cover Design: Cynthia Akiyoshi
Book Design: Sarah Bennett
Cover Image: iStock/CEFutcher

Library of Congress Cataloging-in-Publication Data
Medea, Andra.
Safe within these walls : de-escalating school situations before they become crisis /
by Andra Medea, M.A.
pages cm
Includes bibliographical references.
ISBN 978-1-62521-518-5 (pb)
1. School violence—United States—Prevention. 2. School crisis management—
United States. 3. Conflict management—United States. I. Title.
LB3013.32.M44 2013
371.7'820973—dc23   2013036515

Maupin House publishes professional resources for K-12 educators. Contact us for tailored, in-school training or to schedule an author for a workshop or conference. Visit www.maupinhouse.com for free lesson plan downloads.

Maupin House Publishing, Inc. by Capstone Professional
1710 Roe Crest Drive
North Mankato, MN 56003

www.maupinhouse.com
800-524-0634
352-373-5546 (fax)
info@maupinhouse.com

Printed in the United States of America in Eau Claire, Wisconsin.
102013   007819

For Julian, wherever he may be.

Contents

Foreword

No matter who you are, what your training is, or what your job is. No matter what population of people you work with—students, teachers, administrators, or counseling clients: Read this book.

Like almost everyone else in our country, I was appalled as the events of December 14, 2012 unfolded in Newtown, CT. The absolute horror of a young man taking the lives of small children and the staff of the school they attended was shocking, to say the least. Unfortunately, as the details of the shooting, and especially the events leading up to the incident, became public, I can't say I was surprised.

My professional experience ranges from working with chronically mentally ill adults in a group home setting to counseling active heroin addicts in a methadone clinic to standing in between suicidal clients and police officers with guns drawn and being asked to defuse the situation. Just as challenging—and sometimes more frightening—I have three daughters at home and two of them are currently teenagers. Reading and applying the principles in this book will give you knowledge that took me 20 years of personal and professional experience to gain.

Safe Within These Walls is not a book about mass shootings, nor is it an attempt at an all-inclusive answer to school violence. Fortunately, the vast majority of violent incidents in schools, or in another workplace in general, don't involve shooting.

Safe Within These Walls is a clearly written and effective manual to help de-escalate agitated individuals. Andra Medea explains the nature of emotional escalation and gives simple techniques that are proven to be effective. From her upbringing in one of the most volatile neighborhoods of Chicago to her professional experience teaching conflict management to a wide variety of professions, Andra Medea's experience and expertise comes through loud and clear in this step-by-step guide to managing emotional flooding and bringing about positive outcomes to potentially violent scenarios. She incorporates the work of recognized experts, including Dr. John Gottman and Dr. Marsha Linehan, the originator of Dialectal Behavior Therapy (DBT).

Throughout this book, you'll read the same question repeatedly—"Would you rather be right or be effective?" If your answer is that you want to be effective, read this book.

Eric Ward, Psy.D.
Executive Director
Family Counseling Service

Introduction

The shooting of 26 children and 6 adults at school in Newtown, Connecticut was a terrible shock, especially to teachers. Across the country educators heard the news and sat down together, thinking through ways to prevent such a tragedy from happening again.

Lynnette Brent of Capstone Classroom and Professional called me in. She is a former teacher, and she'd heard about my work in de-escalation and violence prevention. She'd heard about the Virtual Tranquilizer, a system I'd developed to de-escalate aggressive or violent people. It's used by psychiatric staff, child welfare workers, veterans, jail personnel, even judges and lawyers. Lynnette wanted to know if this technique could be brought to teachers.

This book is the result. We don't cover just shootings, but the spectrum of aggression that leads to violence. The earlier we intervene with behavior problems, the better the odds of success. The best solution for violence is to prevent it entirely.

I have a personal stake in this; I grew up with shootings in one of the most volatile areas in Chicago. My old high school today has become a national symbol of random, senseless violence.

I grew up at a collision point in history. Martin Luther King Jr. led marches in my neighborhood, which were met by riots. The American Nazi party set up their headquarters two blocks from my home. My mother sided with civil rights, and so I got beat up a lot. In order to survive, I got to be skilled at handling violent people. I observed their ways and learned what made them tick.

When I left the neighborhood I realized I knew more about heading off violence than most people, and that I could teach it. I co-authored one of the early books on women and violence, which sold over 50,000 copies, and developed a form of self-defense called Chimera, which eventually was taught to over 20,000 women. While most of the talented teachers have since moved on, years later they still get calls from students who now want the same course for their daughters and granddaughters. Its success rate was excellent. The technique was based on reading situations and finding solutions where it looked like no options might exist.

This work led me to de-escalation in any sort of conflict. I taught conflict management at Northwestern University and the University of Chicago before developing the Virtual Tranquilizer. The goal is to calm down people who don't know how to calm down themselves.

Let me tell you a secret: Aggressive people don't understand themselves very well. There's nothing more arresting than finally finding the key to reach someone, watching his eyes shift, and seeing the fight drain out of him. For teachers working with troubled students, it's a breakthrough moment we live for.

There's a world of research to inform what we do in de-escalation, but my heart is still with the kid whisperers, teachers who somehow know what to do. I use their wisdom to build on the science, sometimes using research to explain their techniques.

What We Will and Won't Cover

In this book, we'll work from different principles. The first and most important thing is to simply notice. Observe physical cues, notice danger signs, pick up on patterns. You can't change what you can't see. As you get better at reading situations, you'll have the ability to intervene early, before a situation gets completely out of hand.

The next theme is to make the most of windows of opportunity. There are good times and bad times to talk to a kid. There are optimal times to intervene. And even if there is a fight, there's an opportunity to work with the same kids to prevent future incidents. Aggression often smolders for a long time before it erupts into violence. Staying ahead of situations and choosing our moment can greatly improve results.

Finally, we'll learn to work with the brain rather than against it. During conflict, the brain malfunctions in predictable ways. We can use that knowledge to good effect.

This method assumes that you are not a counselor, but a concerned teacher or administrator who needs to manage aggression. The emphasis is practical, here and now, rather than deep and long-term. Counseling may be the next important step, but this is about immediate de-escalation. Even psychologists benefit from these techniques, since it's extremely difficult to get deeper work done when a kid is going off on you.

This book will not cover ground that has already been well covered elsewhere. For instance, we will not cover bullying or substance abuse, because there's so much available already. If you'd like to follow up on related topics, there is an appendix at the end of this book where you can find a list of excellent resources.

We also will say little about physically breaking up fights. Any time you make physical contact with a child, you enter a world of legal and administrative complications. Your local school board has already decided how they want physical contact handled, and rules vary from district to district.

The Virtual Tranquilizer is a non-contact de-escalation technique. Non-contact means less fallout, fewer family confrontations, and fewer administrative headaches. Whatever your local regulations or classroom philosophy, it will never hurt to have non-contact options.

How to Use This Book

Teachers are busy, so this book is compact and easy to use. It's written in plain English, so that it can be used by anyone: new teachers, old pros, administration, even security staff. All staff needs to be on the same side, with enough shared information to support one another.

The first section is an overview of techniques, such as how the brain malfunctions during anger, reading body language, and patterns in escalation. The second section breaks out solutions by age group: K–2, 3–6, middle school, and even parents. Parents can also get aggressive sometimes. The final section looks at mental health options when counseling isn't enough, and finally, what to do about school shootings.

While interventions are broken out by age group, you may want to glance through the full range. For instance, fighting is covered in detail under middle school, but that's obviously not the only time fights take place. Conversely, most of K–2 is about setting up a safe, calm space, but it includes a section on kids emerging as leaders. Leaders with immature judgment can be a great source of trouble at any age. You want to stay ahead of this and guide their ability in positive channels.

In working on this book, I often tapped teacher–mentors that other teachers turn to for advice. They were more than generous in sharing their experiences and wisdom. Since many mentors are older, I also sought out gifted younger teachers for generational balance. Older teachers have great insights, but younger teachers will be taking charge as the older generation retires. Both perspectives are valuable.

Beyond that, I had the benefit of diverse voices from regions across the United States and Canada, urban, suburban, and small-town teachers, of various races and ethnicities, with students who were wealthy, poor, or middle class. Behavioral problems appear across the board, and practical advice needed to reflect that.

Special Thanks

The following are just a few of the many teachers and child specialists who offered their advice.

Virginia Brucker is a primary school teacher with 30 years of experience in a town not far from Vancouver, British Columbia. Her goal was to educate the heart, to build character in order to bring out the best in a child, and to set a child on a path for life.

Virginia has a gift for getting through to kids who other people have given up on. Of course she's extremely intelligent, but what's most striking about Virginia is her heart and her ability to see past the surface. I was fortunate to have Virginia as an advisor and reader on this project. It is a far better book for having Virginia involved.

Zak Mucha, LCSW, is my colleague in developing trainings for psychiatric staff. Zak spent seven years supervising an Assertive Community Treatment (ACT) team in one of the most challenging districts in Chicago. ACT teams work with clients with severe mental illnesses, many of whom refuse medication. ACT staff operate in the community alone, unarmed, and without police backup. Zak became legendary for his ability to de-escalate clients that others would back away from.

Zak and I started working on techniques for this population, adapting and refining Virtual Tranquilizer techniques. Zak patiently described himself as my guinea pig.

About two years ago, we started training other mental health workers in this de-escalation approach. We called it No Contact, No Drug (NCND) De-escalation, because the alternatives for people with mental illness having an aggressive episode were either to be wrestled into restraints or to be given powerful sedatives. A non-force option was dearly needed.

Zak, in action, is frankly phenomenal. It's been an honor to work with him.

Lynnette Brent is the product manager at Capstone responsible for getting this book underway. Lynnette is an ex-teacher, and she knew from her work in the trenches what teachers need and how they want to hear it. She was patient, smart, and determined to see that teachers get the resources they need. Lynnette did without a lot of sleep to get this book done.

Cheri Colburn was the editor who came with the reputation for being formidably tough, with a great eye for detail. I expected her to be a fine editor, but was pleased to find the way she cared about kids and the teachers who work with them. Her heart and good judgment is evident throughout this book.

David Willette and Mary McCarthy led the marketing team charged with getting this project out where teachers could find it. You're reading this now because David, Mary, and their colleagues at Capstone found a way to get it to you.

To the many other teachers and advisors who helped, thank you for your patience and your faith in this work. I hope it's worthy of you, and I hope we can do something good for the kids out there.

Names and identifying details have been changed in all stories and examples. Any errors in the interpretation of teachers' or researchers' work are entirely my own and do not reflect on the experts cited.

– A.M.

CHAPTER ONE

Adrenaline Overload

U pset kids get into trouble. Sometimes they fight. They may be upset from problems at home, in the neighborhood, or with each other. They may get into fights over nothing or next to nothing, fights in which they lose their heads and do things they may later regret, involving you, the principal, or possibly the police.

That's why it's important to know about *flooding.*

Flooding was named by a researcher, Dr. John Gottman, who studied how people fight. He discovered a key finding: When people are stressed, a wash of adrenaline floods the brain and physically disrupts circuitry. This change explains many of the exasperating behaviors we see in troubled kids, and it blocks our best efforts to help.

The Virtual Tranquilizer approach assumes certain circuits will be blocked and works around them.

Talking to a Wall

Angry kids don't listen.

Sometimes it's like talking to a wall. Nothing gets through. You try telling them something they need to know, something that will help them, perhaps something they desperately need to hear. You may as well have been talking to the cabinet in the corner.

One study found that this adrenaline overload—flooding—disrupts the part of the brain that takes in new information. It isn't that these kids are ignoring you. It's that they can't absorb what you say. When they are flooding, that part of their brains is essentially disconnected.

This phenomenon was so marked that the same researchers thought to test it on scientists, who, after all, are trained to pick up information. They put scientists in the lab, brought them to a state of flooding, and then brought new information into the room. Not only did the scientists not notice the new information, *their skin* didn't respond. The disconnect is that profound.

So, in fact, you could wear yourself out trying to get through to these kids, who still will not hear you. You could lose your temper and yell, up the threats and try to shock them, even stay up nights trying to think of some combination of words that might finally work. And you may feel baffled that your best efforts have so little effect.

What you'll need to do instead is to shift the adrenaline so they *can* hear you and then try to talk with them. At that point, perhaps, you can get somewhere.

Magnification

Another problem is that adrenaline magnifies; it particularly magnifies threat. Parents see this at home. The parent says, "Put down the cell phone and do your homework." The kid says, "You don't want me to have any friends!"

The parent says, "You'll still have friends. Go do your homework!" The kid says, "You're just trying to ruin my life!"

Parent says "X." Kid hears, "X times 1,000." The scene quickly moves to tears, shouting, slammed doors, and a singular, crashing headache. Decidedly little homework gets done.

A similar dynamic sometimes plays out at school. One teacher found a middle school student had plagiarized his paper. It was clearly taken straight off the Web. It used the vocabulary of a professional journalist, and it took the teacher less than five minutes to find the original article.

The teacher sat down with the student and explained the seriousness of plagiarism. The kid had never heard of it. The teacher explained that this was the kind of thing that was not tolerated, and how he'd get thrown out of college if he ever tried it there. He got an F and had to write a new paper.

The middle-schooler went home in tears, convinced his teacher was going to have him kicked out of school (magnification). The parent showed up incensed. Her kid was in tears, the teacher was threatening to expel her child, and all this *after* he had turned in his work. The parent was livid.

Obviously none of the lesson on plagiarism got through. Now the teacher tried to explain plagiarism to the parent, who was furious and flooding. This worked about as well as it had with the student. Nothing got through; the parent continued to escalate and stormed out of the classroom to find the principal. The situation spiraled into a huge mess.

The upset student could not take in basic information, much less a sophisticated concept like plagiarism. The parent couldn't take in the explanation either, or even the simple fact that her child was *not* being expelled. You'd think the parent would be pleased to hear her son wasn't being kicked out, but not even that message got through.

Both the child's brain and the parent's brain had been hijacked by flooding. Neither of these conversations worked. And they weren't going to work until the flooding was under control.

Signature Signs of Flooding

Many of the signs of high adrenaline describe the behavior of your most trying students. While flooding, people are:

Highly reactive. They may be like walking land mines, ready to explode at the slightest provocation.

Unable to settle down. These kids are all over the place, doing everything except what you asked.

Clingy. They may be tugging on you, flagging you, needing constant reassurance.

Unfocused/Scattered. They seem to have the attention span of mayflies. Anything and everything distracts them.

Physical Symptoms of Flooding

In order to stop flooding, you first have to recognize it. You can't fix what you can't *see*.

With flooding, light-skinned people go red. Dark-skinned people get darker. Sometimes, in pale children, you might see them go white, and then red. You are watching the effects of chemicals washing through the child.

Kids who are flooding are apt to have clumsy, jerky movements; they lose their small muscle coordination. They may knock over their juice, knock into each other, or knock things off your desk.

Never yell at a child who has just spilled something with those signature jerky movements. Her adrenaline's already too high. If you snap at her, her adrenaline will spike. So now she will jump up, knock over her chair, bump into the kids next to her, make twice the mess, and have other kids in tears.

If you see these outward effects, it's a sign that this kid's brain is malfunctioning. She may be volatile and overreact. At this moment she won't be able to listen or learn, so scolding won't work.

Have her take some deep breaths; have her run and get some towels to help you clean up the mess. All of this will help burn down adrenaline and get everyone back on track. Talk with her afterwards, *after* she's calmed down.

Behavioral Signs of Flooding

Pressured speech These kids sound overexcited; words are pouring out. They can't get the words out fast enough, and they're shouting over each other to get your attention. Young kids may physically jump up and down or tug at you.

You'll notice that they can't really hear what you say. You have to say it several times—"Settle down! Settle down! Settle down!"—because they didn't hear the message.

They may be happy and overexcited, but this is still adrenaline overload. For instance, as they're jumping around, their movements are big and jerky. And even if they're happy at the moment, when kids are over-stimulated, things can quickly shift to temper and tears.

Another factor is that flooding is contagious. If they're jumping and shouting at you, it's likely to get on your nerves. If *you're* shouting to get their attention, you actually add to the overload. You're now cycling and escalating together.

At times like this, don't try using words at all. The language part of the brain is impaired, so gestures work better. For instance, if you want to get a jumping passel of kids to calm down, spread your arms like a conductor. Then smoothly lower them, like a conductor signaling the orchestra to bring down the volume.

This works within the limitations of the flooding brain. Work with the brain, rather than against it. Since it's hard to get through with words, fall back on visual cues.

Mirror Neurons

When a child is flooding, visuals work better than words. For best effect, model the behavior yourself. For instance, if you want them to take a deep breath, *you* take a deep breath. If you want them to lower their voices, *you* lower your voice. Showing works better than telling.

Of course, the behavior you model will carry more weight than what you say. But you're also making use of mirror neurons.

You've heard the expression, "Monkey see, monkey do." It's a not particularly polite way to describe something valid about the way the brain works.

Mirror neurons have us mimic what we see. And the more excitable we are—the more adrenaline takes over—the more powerful the effect of mirror neurons.

For instance, picture sports fans caught up in a football game on TV. Their adrenaline's high—they're really into it. Their eyes are fixed on the screen. The running-back grabs the ball and darts to the left— the fans jump to one side in their chairs. The running-back gets hit— the fans jolt, as if they were hit.

The fans never leave their chairs, but their bodies mimic the moves of the player. These are mirror neurons at work, and adrenaline heightens the effect. A bored or casual observer doesn't react this way. But the viewers who are intense and emotionally excited will dodge and weave in their chairs.

In a classroom, you want mirror neurons working for you. If you want someone to slow down and take a deep breath, *you* slow down and take a deep breath. Make it visible and say as much: "Whoa, whoa. There's a lot coming at me. I just need a deep breath. C'mon, you do it too."

Then visibly take a deep breath. Make it a broad gesture. If they see you do it, they'll do it. If they don't see you do it, they are far less likely to draw that breath and physically calm down.

Bringing a Kid Out of Flooding

Teachers have long known that deep breathing helps kids calm down and helps them get their tempers under control. There are dozens of different ways to get them to do it, and we'll cover a list of them by the end of the chapter.

Another way to drop adrenaline is to work the large muscle groups. The large muscles are the arms, legs, back, and torso. The diaphragm is also a large muscle, which may have something to do with the way that deep breathing works.

If you want to get through to a kid who's angry, upset, or over stimulated, first give him a physical activity that works the large muscles. You might have him walk up and down the stairs three times, or help you move a desk: "Samuel, I need some help. Give me a hand with this."

Some teachers send overwrought kids across the building to deliver a note. You can also have them do isometrics, like pushing their hands together or pushing hard against the wall. Researchers have even found that kids test better if you have them dash up and down the room before the test.

With older kids, you might give them two laps around the athletic field. The protocol is to have them first burn through some adrenaline, and talk afterwards. That gives you the best chance of getting through.

The Assistant Principal

Large muscle action also works well on kids fresh from a fight.

This story came from Judi Kosterman, Ph.D., who at the time was an assistant principal. As assistant principal, she got the kids who had just been fighting. The kids would come in, still jumping with anger. At first, there was no getting through.

Kosterman was a small woman, and she kept a stack of heavy books on the counter. As the fighters came in, she'd say, "We need to talk! But first I need your help with something. Help me move those books."

The kids would pick up the books, and she'd start talking with them, as they stood there holding the heavy stack of books. Well, this was isometrics, working the core muscles in the torso. After a while their eyes would clear and they'd start to settle down, and soon they'd start to tire.

They'd say, "Miss, where did you want these?" And she'd have them put the books back on the counter. By then, they'd burned through enough adrenaline, they'd calmed down, and they could talk.

Kosterman used this trick for *nine years* without anyone noticing that they put the books down exactly where they found them. Well, short-term memory loss goes with flooding, so they didn't remember where they got the books. Flooding people are also suggestible: in nine years' time, every kid who was asked to do so picked up the stack.

Now, after awhile, repeat offenders might have known if they were sent to the assistant principal she'd put them to work. That's fine. They also would have learned that when they got into her office, they'd start to settle down and perhaps feel better.

Flooding—and flood control—is learned behavior. The past experience of going to her office and calming down meant in the future it was easier and faster to calm down. The more they repeat the protocol, the faster it works. These are cumulative gains.

Kosterman never knew why this business with the heavy books worked. She learned it from watching her mother deal with her sister through a stormy adolescence. Instead of getting into an awful fight, the mother had the sister pick up something heavy or help her with something strenuous. Then, once the adrenaline burned down and the sister's eyes cleared, they'd finally sit down to talk.

There's one common sense caveat with this: never hand an angry kid something small enough to throw. Appropriate choices might be a stack of books, a pre-packed moving box, or even loading them up with volumes you pull out of a shelf. You want something large enough to fill both arms to work the central torso. And, of course, make sure the weight is appropriate for the child.

How to Tell It's Working

In order to gauge when it's time to talk, you have to be able to tell how things are working.

The assistant principal watched the students' faces to gauge if they were calming down: their eyes would clear. As one teacher put it, "They'd come back into their eyes."

Most of the visual cues that alert you that someone is flooding, such as a red face or uncoordinated motion, do not work as well in helping you gauge them coming out of flooding. For instance, the red face may only gradually go back to normal. The lack of coordination may stay with them for a while.

Apart from the difference in the eyes, listen to the voice. For instance, a kid who is flooding often has that rapid, pressured speech. Her words tumble over each other, as if she can hardly talk fast enough to get the words out.

As the kid comes out of flooding, her speech returns to a more normal, conversational speed. It's not pressured, like a fire hose; it's more like a normal flow.

Some students who are flooding may not be able to get words out at all. If they have a stutter, the stutter will get worse under flooding. Their speech may lock up entirely. As they start to come out of flooding, a few words might come out, and then a few more. And gradually, normal speech resumes.

The quality of their speech also changes. For instance, while flooding they may speak in disjointed sentences: breaking off words, stumbling, doubling back, or repeating themselves. The language centers are affected by flooding, and it makes people incoherent. As they come out of flooding, they'll talk in more complete sentences, and their thoughts will make more sense. Their words will be more organized. It's easier to follow what they're saying, and perhaps, at this point, you can finally find out what happened.

Flooding as Learned Behavior

Kosterman trained the kids to calm down while they were in her office. With more experience, they came to expect that they would calm down in her presence. Other administrators, with a different approach, often had the opposite effect.

Kids learned, after going to her office, that she would probably put them to work. They also learned that she was relatively easy to talk with. They came away feeling more in control of themselves, even if they got a detention.

As you start working with kids on flood control, they will start learning what to expect. Eventually, they will start calming down *before* they reach you, at the sight of your door or even on the way down your corridor.

Flooding attaches to sights and sounds. Usually this works against us: If Joel flooded the last time some kid mouthed off to him, he will start to flood again when he sees the same kid, even if the kid isn't giving him trouble this time.

The door to the principal's office may trigger flooding in a kid who has been sent there for punishment. It will have no trigger for a kid who was sent there to deliver a message. If a kid is sent to deliver a message a few days after being sent for punishment, his heart will likely start racing getting closer to the door, even though he hasn't been sent for punishment. The sight of the door is associated with flooding, and the body reacts accordingly.

Calm can also be associated with sights and sounds. You want your space and the sound of your voice to be associated with calm. You know teachers who do this already, and kids begin to settle down even as they enter her room.

This isn't magic. It's the benefit of learned behavior. You want it working for you, rather than against you.

Consequences and Distraction

Half of what we do in school is to teach about consequences: the consequences of punching another kid, or the consequences of not studying for a test. But once flooding comes into play, consequences don't work as well as we might hope.

Flooding interferes with the part of the brain that deals with consequences.

As you know, the part of the brain that processes consequences isn't fully developed in young people. Add flooding, and the child is operating under a double handicap.

You may have talked to a quick-tempered kid any number of times about consequences. Yet when he's angry enough, consequences disappear. Later, you might ask him about those long talks you had, he might bite his lip or shrug. He can't explain what came over him.

You might think the answer is to give him more consequences, but if consequences didn't work the first few times, maybe that's not the only answer. Instead, try working with distraction. While consequences are impaired at the point of flooding, distraction increases. You can use this to stop a fight.

Let's say Sara has a nasty habit of exploding at teachers. At that moment, she sees red, and consequences vanish. Encourage Sara to come up with a physical strategy, such as, "When I feel I'm about to go off, I will press both hands into my desk. Hard."

Mr. Hugo in science lab may be mystified by Sara pressing her lab bench into the earth, but that's OK. If it helps Sara stay out of detention, it's good.

You want the kid to pick out her own strategy, the technique that feels best to her. She will need it to fall back on when she's seriously under pressure, so you want it to be a good match.

The Violent Impulse Is Fleeting

Dr. Charles Bell, who did landmark research on violence, pointed out that the actual impulse to violence is fleeting. Anger or aggression may build a long time, but the urge to act is brief. In fact, it may be regretted immediately afterwards. Miss that moment, and the fight may not happen. Kids can pull themselves back from the edge.

Our job is help kids miss that moment. Many of the feelings may still be there, but missing the moment is a huge step forward. Anything we try to accomplish with kids is easier if they're not exploding or spending half their time in detention.

The problem isn't just how to lower adrenaline; something as simple as deep breathing does that. The problem is how to get a kid to take that deep breath at a moment when every fiber of his being wants to punch some other kid. It's the timing, not the action.

Consequences tend to be remembered at the wrong time. Regrets aren't especially helpful when you're already on suspension. But distraction spikes at the moment of flooding, when the kid is rushing towards trouble. We can make use of that.

You may see a kid struggling with whether to punch a kid or not, yearning for it, yet with a flicker of awareness that there will be bad consequences. You might see him physically shift back and forth, torn between giving in or not. Our job is to prepare the kid to tip the balance.

Know Your Own Symptoms

For a kid to catch herself when she's about to snap, she needs to recognize the signs that indicate she's about to lose it. The earlier she notices them, the better her odds to prevent it. So part of the strategy is to teach her how to recognize the physical or mental cues that precede an outburst.

Sometimes the first red flag is that your head starts pounding. It may feel like a tourniquet tied around your head, or like your head is going to explode. It may be a headache that starts on one side and starts to take over your head.

Another sign is that your breathing goes short. You may feel like you can't breathe, like the walls are closing in, like you want everyone away from you, or that you need some air. You may feel like you've got to get outside. In fact, at this point, some kids will bolt from the room or shove other kids away.

Your heart starts racing. It may feel like it's pounding so loud someone else can hear it, like it's throwing itself against the walls of your chest.

Some people have their mouth go dry, a "cotton mouth" feeling. Some others get tingling in their fingers and toes. Some people's hands feel light, as if they could float.

There may be a surging feeling like a tidal wave that will smash everything before it. These are all signs of flooding.

There are different ways to manage this. For instance, if you feel the walls are closing in, it can help to step to the window and look outside. Pick out a tree and count the branches. It will feel like you've gotten more space. Or instead of shoving someone else to get space, step back. If stepping back feels like too much of retreat, step to one side. But keep your priorities in order. It's important to deal with the flooding first, and deal with anyone else later.

Mental Signs of Flooding

Some people may notice the physical signs first while others may find it easier to pick up on the mental signs.

If you're flooding, you may notice that your thoughts start whirling, so you can hardly think. It may feel like there's just too much coming at you. Or you may feel overwhelmed, like everyone's pushing at you.

You may feel quick-tempered, prickly, as if it would take very little to set you off. Other people irritate you—all of them. Or you may just feel like you've had enough.

Any red flag will do. The key thing is to notice your own signs of flooding.

Teachers

After going over these last lists of symptoms, it may have occurred to you that you feel this way too, at times, especially on days when the kids are getting on your nerves.

Flooding doesn't happen just to kids. It happens to teachers too. And worse, it's contagious. So on the days when the kids are fussing and fighting and driving you crazy, your thoughts will start whirling, and you get that telltale headache when you've just had enough. This means your brain has started to malfunction. You may have the same symptoms that troubled kids have: building anger, overreacting, and distracted, scattered thinking.

If you see that kids are flooding, check if you're flooding too. If you are, you'll have to do some flood control. The same rules apply to you: Your job is to manage your own flooding first, then deal with anyone else.

If you want kids to manage flooding, you'll need to model these behaviors yourself.

Apart from deep breathing, or lifting something heavy, here are some other ways to ease flooding.

Humor

Laughter drops adrenaline levels. You've seen tense situations where someone made a joke and broke the tension. Everyone laughed, and it all blew over. Laughter dropped the adrenaline, and distraction kicked in; they all went on to something else.

Of course, use common sense. Kind humor de-escalates aggression; nasty humor is a form of provocation. Be kind or leave humor alone.

Singing

Singing drops adrenaline. For your kids, any simple song will do. You might even have them sing snatches of a ditty before a test.

Silly songs work well. You can find them online or make up your own. For older grades, you can have them make up a song based on a familiar tune.

For older kids, rap songs may or may not work. Rap has a chanting rhythm, which is compelling, but doesn't involve deep breathing the way that conventional singing does. Experiment, and see what works best for your kids.

The following is a song for teachers or administrators, offered by a contributor who wished to be known as a "Reforming Maniac." It is sung to the tune of "I Won't Grow Up" from Peter Pan.

> *I won't blow up (I won't blow up)*
> *I don't wanna be a fool (I don't wanna be a fool).*
> *And snap at other people*
> *Like they were just some tool.*
> *Cause blowing up means I will be*
> *By myself sitting in a tree.*
> *I won't blow up. Not Me!*

Repeat as needed.

The Clapping Game

This is a call-and-response clapping game that can be used to break up impending fights. It's easiest if you teach this game ahead of time, but it's such an infectious game, it can work on the spot.

It goes like this: The teacher claps twice and gestures for the kids to do the same. They clap twice. Teacher claps three times. Kids clap three times. Teacher claps four times, breaking up the rhythm. Kids clap four times, matching the rhythm.

Teacher keeps switching the rhythm and count, slapping a knee, and making it complicated enough that the kids have to concentrate to mimic the pattern. Keep it up, moving different parts of the body, until the tension is broken and kids have forgotten about fighting. It could also be used to break the tension before a test.

I learned this game from Mariana Garrettson, a research scientist with the Injury Prevention Research Center at UNC Chapel Hill, who also teaches Virtual Tranquilizer on occasion. The technique is used in domestic violence centers. The thing is, kids are thrown into shelters because there's been a violent incident at home. They're scared, completely disrupted, and in close quarters with a bunch of other kids who are scared and completely disrupted. And all of them, by definition, have come from families where there's been violence. So it's very easy for a fight to break out among the kids.

You can feel the tension building or see kids across the room squaring off to fight. The sharp double clap is a piercing sound, quite arresting. In fact, it's used in noisy martial arts studios as the command to stop.

The clapping, using different parts of the body, gets kids moving and burns off adrenaline. The changing rhythm is irresistible—you don't want to be left out. The rhythm taps the power of cognitive dissonance—your brain wants to complete the pattern to resolve the dissonance.

The clapping game uses no words, but it requires concentration to follow the count and the pattern. If a kid loses the pattern, a kid right next to him will get it right, so the first kid will concentrate harder. Kids focus on keeping up, and they forget about the fight.

The game is contagious and compelling, and it completely breaks the tension. By the end, kids are laughing as they manage to keep up and feeling unified by clapping all together as one. The fight is forgotten.

This method works best in enclosed spaces, like a classroom, where tensions can build towards explosion. It's contagious enough to travel across the playground, but it's best in closed spaces.

Once you teach this game, it can be the cue for kids to drop whatever they're doing and mimic the clap. It's handy to use if you feel an explosion coming.

Non Sequiturs

People ramping up for aggression are typically rushing down a narrow track. Saying something completely unexpected can work to jog their brain off track.

One teacher, Miss Plathe, had a child in her class, Jonathon, who was taller than she was. He wasn't a bad kid, but he was in a tough stretch. He came in one morning spoiling for a fight and saw the teacher in the coat room. He said, "Miss Plathe, you are the worst teacher I ever had."

This was first grade. Plathe primly nodded, "Thank you, Jonathon." He did a double-take; then they both burst out laughing. It was wildly not what he expected. And they both went on to have a very good day.

A variety of unexpected diversions can work. As the tension ramps up between two kids, you can call, "Sam, quick: four times four. Sam, think: four times four!" Sam will likely look somewhat dazed; if he's flooding, the parts of his brain that handle both math and short term memory won't be working.

Before Sam gets too embarrassed, call to the other one: "Michael: what's the capital of Florida? We just covered it in geography, capital of Florida! It starts with...!" You'll now have two young fighters unsure if they should answer your questions, or go back to squaring off. Keep them distracted and separate them: "Sam, look up the table: four times four. Michael, go to the computer, find me the capital of Florida. Back here in four minutes. Go!"

The orders are short and designed to distract students and keep them off balance. Keep this up: Physically separate them, and keep them occupied with their eyes off each other. By the time they get back to you with answers, the tension should be broken and they may have forgotten what they were going to fight about.

By the way, drug rehab counselors reported using non sequiturs when clients were escalating and nothing else was working. The counselors didn't know why it worked and were surprised to hear that other counselors had hit on it too. Since it seemed to make no sense, no one thought of discussing it.

A possible explanation is that a verbal or visual surprise cues a part of the brain that deals with incongruities. Typically, the person's eyes flutter or shift to the side, his jaw drops a bit, and he looks like he's searching his mind. These are signs of brain activity. In any case, when he comes back to attention, the angry mood is broken. He's in a different place.

There are reasons I mention the likelihood of brain processing. First, during that pause, his brain is busy. Give him a few moments to do this. Don't ask questions, don't interrupt. You want him to do what he's doing.

Second, remember that surprise is key. Surprise would be the factor that would spark the engagement of a different part of the brain. So, unlike other forms of flood control, a complete non sequitur can't be used over and over again. Most techniques get better with repetition, as students learn to work with you to manage flooding. But this one doesn't work with repetition.

If, two weeks later, you again throw a complete non sequitur at the same angry kid, it may not work. That's because it's no longer a surprise. Now it's just annoyance.

Special Tips to Help Kids Calm Down

These are some great tips from Danielle Van Vliet, a school counselor.

For Younger Kids

The imaginary balloon Have the angry kid imagine blowing up a balloon. The balloon is the size of the problem. So a big problem would require blowing a big balloon, a humongous problem a huge balloon.

Thing is, nobody wants a small problem. So this gets the kid to do some serious breathing. It also takes focus off whatever it is the child is angry about.

Also, with time, the child will learn to gauge his own anger: after a few rounds, every balloon won't be gigantic. They'll start coming in different sizes. Remember, flooding magnifies, so at first every problem is gigantic. It's a step forward when the child can notice and gauge the difference.

Hot soup breath Another technique is to have the child imagine holding a bowl of delicious hot soup. It smells great, but it's too hot to eat. Have him put the imaginary soup in front of his face and inhale the delicious smell. Now blow to cool the soup. Then inhale the wonderful smell, and blow to cool the soup. Apart from the breathing, the image helps to break visual focus.

Little cars Have the kid who's very angry lie on the floor on his belly. Put down a little toy car, and have the child blow the car to a certain point across the room. (Tell the child to imagine the car is hot and he or she needs to blow it away.) Between the deep breathing and swimming along the floor, that kid will get a full work out.

Six-sided dice Take a large, toy dice with six blank sides. Ask the child for six things that would relieve her feelings. Write them on the six sides with a dry erase marker. Then have the child roll the dice. Whatever comes up is what she'll do.

For Older Kids

This method works if the kid has a cell phone or an MP3 music gadget, like an iPod. Have the kid record her own voice, telling herself whatever works for her: silly songs, calming sayings, a "safe space" meditation, whatever. An older kid may be resistant to hearing an adult talk her down. If so, have her record her own voice saying the things she needs to hear.

Then, let's say she's on the playground, and a situation is getting to her. She can put in her earphones and her own voice will cue her to calm down. From the outside, she will look like a cool kid, aloof from the uproar. From the inside, she's working on her turmoil.

Anger Follows Vision

If you need to separate two kids who are about to fight, you want them out of each other's sight. This isn't just so they can't provoke each other. Flooding attaches to sights and sound. Anger can attach to whatever the person is staring at. If you control the sightlines, you can control the fight.

For instance, if you see two kids getting angry with each other, you can say, "Jeffery, this way. I need you over here." You can take him to a hallway, around the corner, anywhere where he can't see the other kid. Once he is separated from the other kid, have him do something physical: "I need you to get this equipment down." Have him move something heavy, but not breakable. His small muscle coordination may be off, so moving old books or gym gear could work. This is not the time to move laptops or the fish tank.

Go back and do the same thing with the other would-be fighter: move him so he can't see the first student. Don't let them back in each other's sight until they've had time to work their muscles and settle down.

This is easy to do on the playground, where's there's physical space to direct kids: "Jeffery, top of the slide. Now!" "Eric, I want to see how fast you can run to the corner and back. Now! Go! Faster!"

Gym teachers can be great at this. They can readily send kids off to opposite ends of a field, or have them do five push-ups quickly.

You're making use of the fact that flooding people are easily distracted and suggestible. This is manageable *once you break their eye contact with each other.* But you can't get through if their eyes stay magnetically locked on each other. Disrupt eye contact first.

A warning here. Anger follows vision. If you've intervened to break up a fight, you may suddenly find both kids have turned that anger on you.

Well, when they were both flooding, their rage was focused on each other. But once you stepped into the middle, both pairs of eyes focused on you. Consequently, they can both become angry with you, even though you had nothing to do with the original conflict.

This is why you distract the kids by giving them something else to focus on, like moving equipment or running to the slide and back. Keep them moving, and don't let them near each other until they've have time to burn off some adrenaline. Talk it over with them later, when you have better odds at getting through.

Would You Rather Be Right or Be Effective?

In this chapter we've covered a long list of ways that flooding—adrenaline overload—interferes with the brain and wreaks havoc with behavior.

In managing behavior, teachers and administrators resort to different tools: discipline, talks, yelling, threats, and possibly, eventually jail.

But consider what happens as we yell and threaten: Adrenaline rises. The angrier we get, the more we spike these kids' adrenaline. If adrenaline is behind the problem, then you are doing the very thing that will get you more of the behavior you don't want.

I'm not saying you're not entitled to be angry; I'm saying it's a lot less productive than you'd think.

I'm also not saying that you renounce all disciplinary tools and let kids run over you. Instead, consider adrenaline as an invisible player in the room. It's a third party that will disrupt your best efforts. You must take it into account if you want to get results. Virtual Tranquilizer skills are designed to do just that.

Adrenaline disrupts behavior and thwarts adult authority. But it's a chemical, not a character flaw. You have to work around it, even when your own adrenaline is urging you to throw a fit.

Educators are faced with a choice: would you rather be right or be effective? Of course you can yell at a kid who's already jumping with adrenaline. You may have every right to do so. You can argue and punish and still get nowhere—because adrenaline is blocking your words. And adrenaline won't listen to you until you lower your voice.

Adrenaline is a great mischief-maker, but there are ways around it. No doubt, it's thwarted you in the past, but it doesn't have to stay that way.

Now that you know how adrenaline hijacks the brain, you can help your students recognize and manage its effects. In doing so, not only will you be able to manage behavioral problems more effectively, you can manage your own pressures better. This will help create a climate that is far more conducive to helping kids grow, learn, and mature into healthy people.

Summing It Up:
High Points of Chapter One

Classroom discipline issues are often affected by adrenaline overload, also called *flooding*. Too much adrenaline physically disrupts brain function. Virtual Tranquilizer skills are practical ways to work around this problem. It's chemistry, not character.

Signs and Symptoms of Flooding

Cognitive signs of flooding include: an inability to take in information, magnification, rapid escalation, and problems with impulse control and weighing consequences.

Behavioral signs of flooding include: overreacting, being quick to take offense, being overexcited and having difficulty settling down, and being clingy and needing continual reassurance.

External signs of flooding include: red or darkened face; jerky, clumsy movements; pressured speech; and disjointed sentences.

Internal symptoms of flooding include: headache, short, shallow breathing, pounding heart, and the feeling that you need more space.

Managing Flooding

To bring kids out of flooding: Have them breathe deeply and work large muscle groups, including the arms, legs, back, and torso.

Specific techniques include: Sending the kid on an errand, humor, singing, or making up ridiculous songs.

Show, rather than say. Flooding people are suggestible, and may readily imitate you. Tap mirror neurons for maximum effect.

To tell that flood control techniques are working, watch for the eyes to clear. Listen to the voice. Speech will become less pressured and more orderly and return to a conversational tone.

Flooding associates with sights and sounds. You want the sight of you, and the sight of your classroom, associated with calm.

continued ...

Teach kids to bring themselves out of flooding. Teach them to recognize their symptoms, then have them pick out a favorite tactic—"If I feel my head is about to explode, I will push my hands together hard."

Be prepared for your own flooding. Flooding is contagious. If chaos breaks out around you, you may go blank. Have your "bag of tricks" prepared in advance, so you don't have to think on the spot.

Flooding and Fighting

Control the line of sight and you control the fight. When two kids are about to fight, disrupt eye contact and separate them. Then give them something physical to do to burn off adrenaline.

Flooding people are easily distracted.

The urge to violence is fleeting. Our job is to help kids miss that moment.

Flooding interferes with the ability to weigh consequences.

Delay "The Talk" until the storm has passed. The time to talk is later, after adrenaline levels drop. The kid will be better able to take in your words, and respond in a more productive fashion.

Overall Guidelines

Adrenaline is a mischief maker, an invisible third party that will disrupt your work with volatile kids. Plan around it.

Would you rather be right or be effective? You can be strictly right and escalate a kid into the principal's office. You can do better.

CHAPTER TWO

Adrenaline Overload and Learning

B y now you may be wondering about the effects of flooding—
adrenaline overload—on teaching itself. Apart from fighting and
disruption, flooding can seriously impact kids' ability to learn.

If kids are flooding, they're noisy and acting out: very little learning
gets done. Students can't concentrate. Things that should be simple feel
hard. And, of course, if flooding spreads to you, you'll become exasperated and be less effective as a teacher.

The following are a few of the many ways flooding can affect students while learning.

Silent Flooding

When we think of flooding, we expect the symptoms to be obvious: the
anxious little girl who keeps popping out of her chair or the youngster
shouting at his classmate. It's adrenaline: fight or flight. But sometimes
kids freeze.

Students can be flooded with adrenaline and yet not act out. In fact,
they may be hardly moving, like the kids who lock up while testing or
the young boy at the blackboard who freezes or the kid who stands up
to speak in front of the class and goes blank.

These kids are experiencing *silent flooding*. They're as upset and
overwhelmed as the kids who are acting out. Their minds are whirling,
emotions are high. But they're not shouting or fidgeting or jumping. In
fact, they're hardly moving. They may not even look at you.

With silent flooding, people may be beset by emotions, but all the
turmoil is on the inside. They're completely locked down. They can't
think, they can't move, and they really can't answer your questions.

Unfortunately, teachers sometimes misinterpret this as willful obstinacy. The lack of response may feel infuriating, and adults may respond by trying to prod the flooding kid into action: "Answer me when I talk to you!" "Johnny! Hello! Earth calling Johnny!" "I'm not going to repeat it again. Look at me! Yes, you. Where is Cairo?"

Do not do this to someone who is silently flooding. It's not that they don't want to answer you. They can't. They can't think, they can hardly move, and they're already doing everything in their power to hold things together. If you keep pushing, anything could happen: They could start yelling for you to leave them alone, that they can't take it, or they could bolt for the door. Whatever your goal may be, it won't get accomplished.

People who are silently flooding may have the signature red or dark face. Their eyes may be downcast or anxiously darting around. Their shoulders may be hunched up, as if they're trying to hide from your words. Sometimes, they may have their arms over their ears, as if trying to physically block out sound.

These are signs of trying to block out stimulation: eyes locked downward, shoulders hunched, ears covered. These kids are on total overload.

Kids experiencing silent flooding can't answer you. They can't learn because they can't take in information. They can't think, organize their thoughts, or do math. Raising your voice does absolutely no good. It only increases the stress.

These students may very well know the answer to the question you are asking, but they won't be able to recall it until they calm down. Lower your voice. Step backwards and give them a little space. Ask something simple, like, "Ellie, do you need a minute here?" Ellie may be able to go as far as nodding her head, yes. Suggest, "Sit down, take a minute, and just breathe. When you're ready, we can take another go at this."

Let Ellie sit to the side, calm down, and clear her head before you give her another opportunity to answer the question.

When kids are hit by silent flooding they're overwhelmed and vulnerable. If you are quietly empathetic and give them time to recover and gather their thoughts, you may win real loyalty.

By the way, to new teachers: this is not an excuse for being "gamed." You don't let Ellie look up the answer when your back is turned. You just let her bring her adrenaline down, so she can function like everyone else.

Problems Sequencing

When kids flood, they lose the ability to sequence. Logic disappears in a jumble of chaotic thoughts. Sometimes there may only be two or three thoughts frantically running in an endless loop. Schoolwork temporarily becomes impossible.

This is why it can be so frustrating to listen to a kid who's upset. She may ramble, stumble, double-back, and then get lost in her own words. Meanwhile, you still can't figure out what the problem is.

And remember, flooding tends to be contagious. So as this kid loses the ability to explain, you lose your ability to follow the story.

Keep your voice low and calm. Then ask some sequence questions: "Just tell me this: What happened first? You were out on the playground and playing tag. And then..."

Once you get the first thing that happened, see if you can find out the second, then the third, and so on, until you have a coherent story.

Because flooding affects the ability to sequence, flooding also disrupts the ability to do math. Math is handled sequentially. Numbers are read sequentially. All of this turns into an awful jumble during flooding. It can do particular damage if a child starts flooding around tests.

Tests

The combination of flooding and tests can be brutal for students. Remember, flooding increases distraction, while tests require focus. Worse, flooding also interferes with short-term memory. Flooding people go blank. The more pressure that's on the kids, the more likely they are to do poorly.

Teachers offer certain standard advice about tests: Come in well-prepared. Get a good night's sleep. Don't leave your studying for the last minute.

We equate being well-prepared with being calm, but that's only true for some of us. Whether students are prepared or not, flooding can wreak havoc with test scores.

When this happens, stress skyrockets so that it's even harder to function. And, of course, flooding is a learned behavior, so if a student humiliated himself on the last test, he'll be stressed when he sits down for the next test. Suddenly a capable student, one who has successfully tutored classmates, goes blank on the test.

Another way flooding impacts test scores is that it interferes with the brain's ability to pick out information. Students cannot see what's directly in front of them. You've probably experienced this yourself. Let's say you're running late and need to find your keys. You tear your house apart looking for your keys, only to have someone else walk in and pick them up from right in front of you.

Your keys were in full view the whole time, but your brain couldn't pick out the image. In class, you've probably had students answer questions on a test that are totally different from the questions that were asked. Their answers may be accurate, but they are unrelated to the actual questions. Their eyes did not pick out the information.

Teachers tend to think this kind of error is about not paying attention to detail. The standard advice is, "Read each question carefully." In fact, it's not necessarily about reading carefully at all; it's a brain malfunction. Under stress the brain may see something different than what's on the paper.

Flooding students may overlook questions or entire sections of a test, which can be fatal to their final scores. Later, when their mistake is pointed out, they're often dumbfounded. They may want to kick themselves. But this isn't about stupidity or carelessness. These are tricks the brain plays when malfunctioning under adrenaline.

If a student has low-level dyslexia, letters or numbers can start moving around at random. The first time they glance at a number it's 1234. The second time it's 1243. The third time it can be different again, and the student can start to panic when the answers don't make sense and double-checking doesn't help.

It's fine to advise your students to read carefully, but you should also make them aware of typical tricks of flooding. The kids are not crazy or inept; these errors are typical of the brain and its quirks.

Teach kids to take a deep breath as they sit down, then another deep breath as they open the test. Have them press their hands together or press down hard on their desks. Not only does physical action help relieve flooding, touching something solid reassures the students that they're not crazy, stupid or hallucinating. It helps ground them again.

Part of the problem is that flooding attaches to visuals or auditory cues, like the sight of a test booklet or the silence before a big test. Sometimes the stress is so intense the air feels thick, as if you could touch it with your hands.

It's all right to say, "Everybody: breathe!" Your students may burst out laughing, That's OK—laughing decreases flooding. You don't want them to get silly, but humor can break tension. Before a test, you can project a cartoon on the wall. Anything that lightens the mood may help their brains function better.

You may also step them through the process, showing them how to stay calm for a test. For instance, you can get them talking: "Today is the day of the big test. How do you feel?" There may be a sudden silence as all those eyes light up with fear. So you coach them: "Feel scared? Feel your heart pounding? What do we do when we're scared of a test?" Walk them through.

The idea is to reverse the established trend and teach them to remain calm before a test. Flooding is a learned behavior, and so is the ability to stay cool under pressure. Tests are part of students' lives now and into the future. If you teach your kids how to control their flooding before and during tests, you have given them a skill that will serve them for years.

Sadly, parents who put a lot of pressure on their kids can actually provoke this response. You've seen how stressed the children of over-achieving parents can be, and they are often some of the most prepared children in the room. That doesn't protect them from going blank or seeing questions that aren't there.

Part of the problem is that children readily absorb the energy around them. If mom is stressed about the child's performance, the child will pick up that stress. This cannot lead anywhere good.

There is a balance to be had. You do not want the kids to be so relaxed and cavalier about a test that they neglect to study. Some children need to be reminded to prepare. Some even need to feel a bit of pressure. But carefully gauge the level of pressure required for kids to perform at maximum ability without shorting-out their wiring.

Self-Regulation

We all have ways of managing our anxieties. You may play computer solitaire. A seventh-grader may check text messages. Texting during homework time can be annoying and counterproductive, but it's a way to manage anxiety. A child who reflexively checks her phone during homework is checking that she's still liked, still connected to her friends. Being connected to friends is one of the most important things in a seventh-grader's universe, so getting that reassurance is a way of soothing anxiety.

A failure to manage anxiety generally makes things worse. For instance, this preteen may be anxious because she's not getting her homework done and her teachers and parents are angry with her. But homework makes her anxious, so she does something soothing, like text her friends. Unfortunately, she's learning that the way to feel better (at least for now) is to avoid her problems and wait until things explode later.

Stress/avoidance is a common loop. It happens everywhere, and it is one reason why it's important for kids to build good habits—so that it's not ruinously stressful to get the homework done and so that the homework builds confidence, not stress.

Balance is the key. This kid, like many others, may benefit from a reasonable amount of anxiety about her grades. The "just right" amount of anxiety will help her get her homework in on time.

Distraction and Schoolwork

We discussed how flooding leaves kids easily distracted. This can cause havoc with schoolwork. Kids already have a short attention span, and flooding can disrupt whatever is left of it. But distraction can happen to anyone, not just kids who spend too much time with social media.

For instance, you may pride yourself on the laser-like concentration that got you through grad school. But you'll notice your focus vanishes when you're running late.

Here's something that happens to many couples: one runs late and one likes to be early. The prompt one will be dressed and standing by the door, fuming. The one who's running late will pick up on the tension from the smoldering one. And suddenly the late one will not be able to get out the door.

Let's say you're the late one. You might start for the door and think, "No, wait, I need to turn off the computer." "No, wait, let me check the iron." "Just one second, let me water that plant." You can hardly believe the kinds of things you simply must do at the last moment, even as your mate is increasingly furious. You need to move 30 feet from your coat to the door, and instead you go ricocheting around the house like a pin ball.

Well, flooding fuels distraction. You start off flooding because you're running late. What's more, you're flooding because your mate is upset, and flooding is contagious. And finally, flooding is a learned reaction for both of you, so the many times you ran late before add to the problem once the pattern's started.

You, who once passed advanced calculus, cannot hold focus long enough to cross your own living room. If this is what flooding can do to you, think of what it will do to an 8-year-old or a hormonal preteen.

Resilience and Trauma

My colleague, Pam Woll, writes and teaches on resilience and trauma, two issues that influence behavior and life skills. Many kids with troubled behavior have been exposed to trauma without having built up the resilience to recover.

Woll defines resilience as the ability to maintain equilibrium under stress and to bounce back from adversity. Trauma is an experience that overwhelms someone's ability to cope.

Woll points out that children acquire resiliency in much the same way they develop muscle: through brief periods of manageable stress, followed by time to recover. If you want an 8-year-old to develop healthy muscles, you don't drop a hundred pound weight on her. You provide small tasks followed by rest, so that the muscle has a chance to develop.

Resilient kids have better coping skills, which means less unhealthy aggression and acting out. While they aren't immune to flooding, they're better at managing their reactions. In the same sense, resilient kids cope better with trauma, but it doesn't mean they're made of steel.

Kids in dangerous neighborhoods get overexposed to trauma. Domestic violence, shootings in the neighborhood, sickness, early death, and everyday casual violence can all result in trauma. For that matter, a disruptive divorce or losing touch with a crucial family member can result in a kind of trauma.

The cumulative effect of repeatedly witnessing or being near violence wears down resilience. This is called weathering: repeated exposure to a background noise of violence, danger, and harm—and the damage this repeat exposure does over time.

Trauma causes changes in the brain that can result in behavior problems. For instance, after exposure to trauma the brain produces less oxytocin. This chemical is related to the ability to bond and trust. Kids exposed to trauma are typically alienated and less trusting of adults. Trauma may also disrupt the brain's adrenaline balance, resulting in a volatile temper.

School is based on basic assumptions on safety, trust, and the reliability of adults. Children who lack the basic chemistry to support trust will be challenging to reach.

Worse, with their trust mechanisms malfunctioning, these kids often choose poorly when they do trust. For instance, they may distrust the school counselor but trust the local drug dealer.

A further complication is that trauma affects the chemical reward system in the brain, the same one that's involved with addiction. So if they don't get the help they need, these kids can be more susceptible to drug and alcohol addictions.

All these symptoms are familiar to teachers. We have seen good kids go bad and turn away from adults. It often happens after trouble at home, the loss of a loved one, or violence in the community. The kids are disrupted. They lose hope and faith in their own future. Researchers now believe this change—an alienation from good influences and a susceptibility for bad influences—is related to a chemical process.

Kids like this are not easy to reach. You need to know you're bumping up against a chemical barrier. You may have known these kids when they were easier to get along with, but then something happened to them or happened right in front of them. Then they started drifting away or getting wild.

When difficult behavior is a result of trauma, threats or punishment don't work as intended. Researchers now think these kids are actually looking for safety, even though they're doing it in a backwards fashion. They're also looking for some relief from stressed and unmanageable feelings.

One solution is to teach these kids about flooding. They are probably living with levels of adrenaline that are high enough to cause physical pain. You will probably be more successful if you talk with them about pain control, rather than anger control.

You may have already tried talking with them about reining in their temper or adjusting their attitude, to little avail. These kids may have no particular interest in changing their anger. They may feel the world heartily deserves their anger, and other people are lucky they restrain themselves as much as they do.

However, if you can teach troubled kids how to drop their pain levels, you will have their attention. They'll be surprised by the relief that comes from flood control, and they may find you a lot more interesting. You can use information about managing flooding as a bridge to get through to them.

Summing It Up
High Points of Chapter 2

Flooding—or adrenaline overload—disrupts classroom performance.

Flooding interferes with learning, ruins test scores, and prepares kids for failure. Plan around it.

Classroom problems include distraction, short-term memory loss (going blank), difficulty with sequencing, difficulty with math, and/or difficulty completing assignments.

Silent flooding is marked by a frozen lack of response. The student is in intense inner turmoil and may hunch down and keep his eyes locked downward in a glossy stare.

Do not prod a child in silent flooding. Don't fire questions at her, and don't crowd her. Take her off the spot and let her gather her thoughts for a moment. She may come out of it by herself, given a moment to calm down.

Flooding wreaks havoc with tests. It affects short-term memory, the ability to register important information, and even the ability to see what's on the test.

To avert flooding before tests tell a joke or have kids race up and down the room or a set of stairs.

Resilience is the ability to recover from life's difficulties.

Trauma is a negative event that overwhelms resilience.

Weathering is repeated, ongoing traumatic experiences, which eventually wear down resilience.

Symptoms of trauma in kids include alienation, disinterest in school or adults, susceptibility to drugs and alcohol, and a loss of hope. Many kids with exposure to trauma display disaffected behaviors, including dropping out, drug use, and problems with the law.

Teach hard-to-reach kids about flooding. It gets their attention.

CHAPTER THREE

Body Language

As we work with upset kids and bump into issues caused by adrenaline, one of the common problems is that words fail. The parts of the brain that handle language become impaired. Words—our stock in trade as teachers and the best ways for us to provide advice and guidance—simply don't work.

It's upsetting and frustrating when words don't work. This, in turn, sparks our flooding, and we're tempted to do things that are unwise: yell, yell louder, yell the same things over and over again, and generally do more of the things that didn't work the first time. Meanwhile, our behaviors are increasing our own and the kids' adrenaline, not lowering it, and we do not get the results we want. In fact, it's more likely that things get worse.

Shouting does not serve us when flooding is at the heart of the problem. And as we've already seen, words don't serve us very well, either. Studies show that under anger or fear, verbal comprehension plummets to 5–25% of the message received. But the rest of the message—75–95%—is absorbed through body language and tone of voice.

This chapter addresses body language and tone of voice. Since that's what's getting through, that's what we have to use. Once you calm the situation using body language, *then* you can go back to talking things through, and then you have the chance to be heard.

Gifted Teachers

Gifted teachers—the kid whisperers—already have a sense of this. Picture for a moment the most effective teachers you have known, those who could control a fractious classroom just by walking in.

These teachers with a sense of command may not be very large. That innate sense of control may be packed into a body that's four-foot-ten. And it isn't necessarily about threat, since these commanding teachers may rarely raise their voice. It's also not about raw energy, since older, more veteran teachers are more likely to have it than high-energy newcomers fresh out of college. But I've yet to hear of a gifted teacher without great skills in body language.

These gifted teachers convey a sense of presence along with deep understanding. Innate wisdom can't be taught, but it is possible to learn how to hold yourself with presence, giving you space to develop the deeper skills of the gifted teacher.

That sense of presence in a teacher calms kids. It provides a feeling of being in good hands. With effective body language, you will have fewer incidents among the kids, and it will be easier to maintain control of your class. The kids will listen to you more. And as you learn to read the signals of others, you will be better able to prevent fights *before* they start, which will make your life much easier.

Nonverbal Cues

Nonverbal cues provide a wealth of information about kids: their mood, attention, receptiveness to your message, and whether or not they're about to kick you.

Your nonverbals also convey information. Your appearance and emotional affect will show whether you like your students, respect them, or dread being in the room with them. They may not absorb the information in a conscious manner. They may not know why they won't listen to you or why they give you a hard time. Kids, especially, absorb impressions and react without really knowing why. How you carry yourself has a great deal to do with the amount of effort it takes to manage your class and your ability to intervene if trouble starts.

In writing this book, I interviewed many kid whisperers and asked what they did that was so different from their struggling colleagues. Repeatedly they'd answer that struggling teachers seemed to miss cues, which gave them trouble reading situations. In fact, the skilled ones were sometimes called mind-readers, because they could pick up on so much by walking into a room.

Moreover, the skilled ones repeatedly mentioned that younger teachers seemed to have particular trouble picking up cues, a difficulty the kid whisperers attributed to social media. Growing up with a screen between you and the person you're speaking with blocks a huge amount of social information. Not being used to receiving and evaluating the full range of social cues can leave you at a disadvantage when dealing with a roomful of kids face to face.

By the way, I interviewed a 20-something with a gift for managing volatile parents. She explained that she had worked in sales since the age of 16. Her sales were face-to-face, which required reading nonverbal cues. She was another one seen as a mind-reader.

If you grew up with social media, or if you supervise those who did, pay particular attention to this chapter. Effective body language and tone of voice are skills that can be learned. It just takes practice.

I first studied body language with a self-defense colleague in Wisconsin. She was tiny and had experience as a graduate student working with gorillas at the University at Madison. Her instructions on entering the primate enclosure were that if gorillas threatened and challenged, she was not to show the slightest fear. She was to stand up straight, square her body, and drop her tone of voice. Consequently, the gorillas would thunder, halt, shrug off their aggression, and go back to munching leaves. It was, after all, just a test. If she stood up well, she could stay.

That posture and the voice of command, used in various ways, can be found among the best teachers, psychiatric staff, judges, and confident, successful professionals everywhere. You want to know these signals and master them.

In this chapter, we'll start with the signals you convey—good and bad—and then move on to discuss reading signals from kids.

Authority Signals

Remember your mentors telling you the importance of good posture, how it made all the difference in the way you were perceived? Well, they were right.

This is authority posture, and it's very similar to what's seen in the alpha ape, the one who leads the troop. It starts with good upright posture—no slouching—and what's called five-point direct stance. The five points are the face, the point of each shoulder, and the point of each hip. Five-point directness has all five points facing the person you're talking to. If any of the five points are turned or twisted away, it indicates uncertainty or weakness.

The full, formal authority face is relatively impassive; there's not a lot of expression to it. It's the stern face of authority.

When working with kids, soften the face of authority: smile. Of course you want to be the leader, but you also want to be a welcoming presence. Kids need to know that you like them and that you're glad they're there. When you need more authority, such as when the class is getting out of hand or you have a fight to break up, take the smile off your face.

The stern face of command is useful when you need to take control of a situation. It's not the face of someone worried about being liked. When things are back to normal and the situation is stable, then please, by all means, smile. Your smile will cue the children that things are returning to normal.

Another sign of leadership posture is taking up appropriate space. This is neither too much, sprawling over the furniture, or too little, shrinking into yourself.

You'll notice the best teachers spatially command the class. The classroom is their space, their territory; they don't hide behind the desk or stay backed against the blackboard. They move freely through the room as if they own it. When you do this, the class is marked as your territory; you are in charge, and kids are secure in your space.

Eyes of Authority

The face of authority also has a direct gaze. Give your students your full attention; don't glance out the windows, look at your feet, or check your cell phone. Your eyes focus on the students and nowhere else.

Children crave full attention, and sadly, it's in short supply. Sometimes adults may be too busy or overwhelmed to simply stop and pay attention. Give your kids your complete and undivided attention, because after all, this is what you expect from them.

Let your approval and affection for them show in your eyes. Smile with your eyes. A fake smile is done with the mouth, and children can spot a fake. Your eyes will keep you honest.

Sister Rita Goedken runs an after-school program in an underprivileged district in Mason, Mississippi. When she first started teaching, her mentor gave her this advice: A class isn't managed with the mouth to speak, but with the eyes to communicate and observe. Kids know they need to look at the teacher. A teacher needs to know how to use that, and she needs to model that same attention with her students.

Sister Rita's mentor would say very little by way of scolding. Instead she would use her eyes to express all her anger or disappointment. Later some kids said in an awed voice, "Oh, Sister, your *eyes*..."

Also, if you express yourself with your eyes, you never say the wrong thing, even when you're flooding. In the heat of the moment, you can say things you wish you hadn't, and once something is said, there's no unsaying it. Because kids are impressionable, you can say something when you are angry that you deeply regret and that leaves a mark on that child. But if you express your anger with your eyes, there is nothing to "unsay."

Another advantage of saying little and speaking with your eyes is that you produce a blank screen. Students will project their own conscience onto that screen. If a student secretly fears that you will march out the door and call his grandma, then that is what he'll see in your eyes. If someone else believes the worst thing is to hold them inside through lunch, then that is what they'll project.

You, of course, have said none of it. You are letting their imaginations run wild. Their consciences will inform them that if they settle down, this terrible fate will pass them by. Deal.

By the way, if you're small and need to fix a direct gaze on a kid who towers over you, step back. You can't fix a powerful gaze while craning your neck straight up. Keep a little distance, and hold yourself as if your gaze is on the same level. The direct gaze, and the way you hold yourself, can convince raucous students that you're at least a foot taller than you are.

Voice of Authority

The voice of authority is low-pitched and resonant. It comes from the chest and carries to the back of the room.

One primary school teacher described the voice as, "firm, but loving." A middle school teacher might describe it as "firm, but warm." Avoid the angry voice; anger will spike adrenaline in your students, and we know where that goes.

Sister Rita put it this way: "I think tone of voice is critical. Kids of whatever age know when they're being respected. Respect shows in your voice. That doesn't mean you're never angry. It means you do not put them down with words or with your tone of voice."

She learned about using her voice effectively from a wise early mentor: "As I listened to her, and I practiced tone of voice, I began to see the difference it made. I'll make use of that voice even when I don't feel like it. I listen to it myself, and it changes me."

The alpha voice is low and resonant. You may, by nature, have a relatively high voice. That's fine. Everyone has both a high register and the low register. Use your low register.

The following voice exercise is taught by the Oklahoma state police. To find your low register, repeat the following:

Ping-pong
Ding dong
Bing bong

"Bing bong" is your low register. Try the same exercise with two fingers pressing on your sternum. As you reach "Bing bong," you should feel your breastbone vibrate. That tells you that you've reached your low register.

If you need to take control of a class or break up a fight or get kids across the room to drop something dangerous, use your low register. It's a voice that will cue students to listen and obey. They often respond reflexively before they know what they're doing.

Perceptions of Authority Signals

Authority signals don't just mean that you'll be heard and obeyed. Using these signals makes it more likely that you'll be trusted, respected, and cooperated with.

People who use calm, confident authority signals tend to be perceived as intelligent, trustworthy, reliable, and worthy of consideration. It will make your life much easier to be perceived this way.

Authority posture also decreases aggression in other people. It's reflex to stop acting out when the alpha steps in. Kids will stop testing you, which means less disruption.

In fact, if you work with kids from military families, they may have trouble taking you seriously if you *don't* display these signals. Military kids sometimes have a reputation for being a bit wild. It's not that they don't respond to authority, but coming from a military culture, they expect more formal signals of authority.

Belligerence Signals

Many adults, when exasperated or angry, shift into belligerence posture: raging voice, furious face, even pounding on the table. The kids shut up and put their heads down. You glower over them. Finally, you feel, you're in charge.

Only it's not true. Authority posture is the sign of the leader who's in charge. Belligerence posture is the sign of someone losing control of a situation. It speaks of losing power. Older kids, especially, might deliberately provoke you just to see you act out.

Belligerence signals happen when teachers have lost it. It can happen to any of us. But belligerence is destructive and needs to be off-limits.

Belligerence has a snarling expression and a crumpled forehead caused by a ridge of muscle over the eyes. Often the jaw is thrust forward, as if ready to bite. (Belligerence is nothing if not visceral.)

There's also a "charging bull" posture, where the head is lowered and thrust forward. This is what's meant by "getting into someone's face." Between the crumpled forehead, jutting jaw, and the head thrust forward, it's almost a bulldog look.

If you see these signals in two kids squaring off, separate them immediately. They're far too close to a physical fight.

Another sign is the hard gorilla stare. The hard stare is a way primates challenge each other to fight. Kids squaring off to fight will drop their heads into that charging bull posture and glare at each other. Some may have their jaws jutting out so far it forces their head back.

Another belligerent signal is shaking your finger in someone's face. Too many schoolteachers do this. Shaking your finger in someone's face happens to be one of the fastest ways to trigger a fistfight in the continental United States.

There was a video that went viral on YouTube of a teacher scolding a student standing with two older female relatives. One relative, we'll presume, was the mom. Mom was not very big, but she clearly didn't like what she was hearing. She had her head down and thrust forward, and her jaw stuck out in bulldog mode.

The teacher, who was not reading cues, shook her finger in the mom's face then looked away. Mom stepped up and punched the teacher full in the face. The teacher never saw it coming.

Never shake your finger in someone's face. And if an adult does these belligerent signs to you, rein in those mirror neurons. Don't display belligerence in response to belligerence. That will only escalate the situation.

To calm things, shift to authority posture. Draw yourself up tall, square your body, and assume a neutral expression. Stop talking. You've nothing to lose; this angry adult is flooding, and she can't hear you anyway. Stop moving. Upgrade to a stony expression. See if the adult doesn't downshift.

Do not model belligerence signals around kids. They'll be more likely to get belligerent around each other when your back's turned. Belligerence also scares kids—which is why they sometimes giggle when they're being yelled at. That's fear bubbling up. Finally, belligerence spikes flooding. So when they put their heads down to read after being yelled at, you can guarantee that no learning is taking place.

Voice of Belligerence

There's a Southern saying: "That's the bark with the bite in it." The voice of belligerence is sharp and staccato with an angry, snarling edge. It could peel the varnish off the doors.

A colleague was once in an airport where a mom was losing her temper with three or four small children. The oldest little boy started off, and Mom snarled, "Jason! Get over here!" Jason flinched, and half the adults within 50 feet flinched, too. That's the voice of belligerence.

The snarling voice inflicts pain. It also means the adult has lost it. You've seen a parent bark, "Dammit! Calm down!" You think that child's calm? The child's adrenaline has just spiked. If the child did shut up, he's on lockdown out of fear.

Everyone loses it sometimes. But if your voice goes sharp and harsh, stop. Stop mid-sentence. Take a deep breath, lower your voice and start over. The snarling voice does harm.

Belligerent signals set students up for failure. Use authority signals to keep order; put belligerence off-limits.

Submissive Signals

Submissive signals cause even more problems than belligerence. People giving off submissive signals often include raw, new teachers hoping desperately to be liked or people who feel overwhelmed. Often submissive signals come from a teacher struggling to keep the class from running wild.

While authority posture stands up straight and takes up space, submissive posture makes the person look almost as if they're shrinking into themselves. Their shoulders may be hunched with the head pulled in, as if they are trying to be smaller than they are.

Instead of the five-point direct posture of authority, some of the five points are twisted or turned away with the submissive posture. The eyes are not calm and steady; they are darting or distracted.

Teachers displaying submissive posture often have an artificially animated face or an ineffectual grin. Of course you want to smile at your students, but this is not a real smile. It's what's called a "fear grin." It's the locked, panicked smile of someone out of their depth.

Submissive posture also includes self-clutching. Teachers may grab their own elbows, wring their hands, or hang onto a book for dear life.

Another submissive sign is fidgeting: toying with your hair, playing with a pen, nervously rubbing a wristwatch or a mustache, or playing with the keys in your pocket. Fidgeting includes anxiously moving around: dancing from foot to foot, fussing with your clothes, and generally looking uncomfortable in your skin.

The teacher displaying submissive posture barely looks in charge. This is not reassuring to small children. It's a disaster around adolescents.

People displaying submissive signals are viewed as weak, stupid, inept, and deserving to be punished. This can bring out the worst in kids. Students don't particularly listen to people displaying submissive signals, so submissive teachers have very little leverage if, for example, they need to break up a fight.

Submissive posture is essentially diminishing. It makes it extremely difficult to keep control of a class.

Submissive Voice

When you're anxious you're also likely to find that your voice goes high and breathy. You sound like a lightweight. Another submissive sign is the upward inflection at the end of each sentence, so that everything comes out sounding like a question: "George, put down that chair?" "Samantha, I want you to start your work?"

In chimpanzee terms, these signals mean, "I'm small, weak, and helpless—don't hurt me." With chimps, it might work, gaining mercy. Humans, perversely, get more aggressive.

To take control when others are flooding; you have to banish all submissive signals. Be thorough. You may have excellent posture and a masterful expression, but overlook a telltale fidget in one hand, and that fidget will give you away. Kids will sense that the rest is a sham.

Pay particular attention to your hands and feet. If you can still your hands and feet, straighten your posture, and convey your strength through your eyes, everything else should fall into place.

To take command without belligerence, take a deep breath and expand your body. Stop moving. Place your hands firmly on the desk, or stand up from your desk. Take charge.

Students and Submissive Posture

The kid displaying submissive posturing is often dismissed as inept or a little "dim." Even worse, submissive signs are associated with dishonesty: fidgeting, shifting, switching from foot to foot, or being unable to look a person in the eye. Americans may assume kids with this posture are lying. In fact, that may not be true at all. A kid with submissive posture may just be afraid of you or daunted by authorities in general.

If the child has gotten it into his head that he just isn't liked by authorities, he may start showing submissive posturing before you even speak to him. You may become convinced he's guilty of something, but you don't know what.

Children who have been chronically bullied often start living in submissive posture, developing a hunched and beleaguered air. They duck their heads, and their voices are breathy and weak. This, in turn, brings out the worst in mean kids.

If you observe that a student has particularly submissive posture, be proactive and talk to the child a little about how to carry himself. And check if someone has been bullying him.

Mixed Signals

Imagine a teacher with an angry 12-year-old in class, a boy with the edgy demeanor of a feral cat. He fronts, barely obeys, and mutters under his breath. But when the teacher comes too close, he physically pulls back, clenches his teeth, and all but holds his breath. When he speaks to the teacher, he has a nervous habit of stroking his hands with his thumb. She sees lots of aggression, but when he thinks no one's looking, he seems to half crouch.

The teacher holds him in for detention one day to try to get to know him. She says, "I've noticed you seem to look fearful. How are you feeling?"

Young feral cat nearly explodes. "Who are you calling a coward? I am not a coward!"

Remember what we said about magnification. So the teacher takes back what she said, apologizes, and says many soothing words. He tells her terribly dangerous stories about himself, trying to impress her. Overall, the teacher gets the impression that her efforts to reach him didn't work.

Well, think about a half-grown feral cat. It's scared of you in the room. But if you say, "Are you afraid, little cat?" it will puff out its fur and arch its back to look gigantic: "I am not a little cat. I am a lion!" And it will then have to prove how fierce and terrible it is.

These are mixed signals, but it's not hard to understand. Saving face is essential for a kid that age. The teacher in the example was right to be careful here and back off—because a kid who actually is afraid may do stupid things to prove he's not.

Would You Rather Be Right or Effective?

The teacher backtracked even though she was right. The kid was tense just being around adults, and he had an edgy, explosive temper. This is consistent with exposure to trauma.

When the teacher asked about fear, he exploded. Of course, she didn't call him a coward, but that wasn't the point. So, she apologized.

She didn't have to apologize, but is it better to be right or be effective? She could be right about which words she used and escalate that kid into detention. Or she could reassure and stabilize him.

This is something easy to forget in the helping professions: because we mean well, we feel we should be taken well, even when we say something upsetting.

If a kid is flashing between belligerence and submissive signals, you need to tread gently.

Euphemisms for Fear

One study found that the fastest way to move a kid from violent to nonviolent is to teach him how to talk about feelings. This is a challenge with a volatile kid. He may be willing to talk about anger in some fashion but be fiercely unwilling to talk about fear. The very implication that he might be afraid sparks an explosion.

If you see these mixed signals, avoid using words like *afraid*, *scared*, or *frightened*. These words could be interpreted as implying weakness or vulnerability, which may feel totally unacceptable. Instead, consider words that imply an element of strength or resourcefulness.

Here are some non-threatening expressions to use when you want to talk about anxiety or fear:
> *A lot coming at you*
> *A lot to deal with*
> *People coming down on you*
> *On your last nerve*
> *Under pressure*
> *Put on the spot*
> *Backed against the wall*
> *Boxed in*
> *Wired*
> *Wrought up*
> *Feeling it*

Phrases like these can be an acceptable way for this student to edge toward talking about his feelings.

Students and Authority Posture

Let's say students have to present in class, a terrifying time for the shy ones. This is a great opportunity to teach authority posture, which is a skill that will serve students in many ways. And, of course, you'll have to model these behaviors, so teaching them will keep you practicing.

Start by having everyone stand up. Then have everyone take a deep breath. Square your shoulders. Look straight out into the room. Drop your voice. Use the same exercise we have used here: ping-pong, ding dong, bing bong.

Ask questions: "What's the right voice?" (Bing bong.) "Where do I look? Do I look at my shoes? Do I look at my fingernails? Where do I look?

Inform the class: "You are the team. You want your teammate to do well. You want your teammate to hit it out of the park because that makes your team look good.

"If, in presenting, a child stands up and freezes, that's OK. You just say, 'Head up. Shoulders back. Deep breath. Now, hit it out of the park!'"

Shaming Signals

The last crucial element in body language is shaming signals. These were identified by researcher, Dr. Albert Sheflen, who studied troubled young people in a psychiatric facility. He videoed their interactions with families and found a disturbing pattern of signals used to shame another; he called these monitoring signals.

Monitoring signals are basically shaming signals, or gestures that show contempt. They operated something like an invisible hand, smacking the kid into line.

Shaming signals include rolling the eyes, mocking humor, smirking, sneering, the "God-you're-stupid" sigh, and a contemptuous sniff.

There tend to be one of two reactions to these signals of contempt. The first is to go ballistic. Older kids especially can be quick to fight when they feel they've been disrespected.

The other reaction is an inward collapse, caving under the shame. The inward collapse we tend to see in unpopular or bullied children. When these kids stand in front of the class to present, the popular kids may smirk or roll their eyes. You can see the unpopular child nearly willing herself to disappear.

If kids respond with rage, they may get into a fight and not be able to exactly explain what came over them. The kid who shamed them, meanwhile, can truthfully say, "I didn't say a thing."

Think of the last time you brought something to class that you worked on a long time. Then some bratty kid rolled her eyes and sighed. Did you feel a flash of rage? And you are an adult, with an adult's self-control. Think of what it does to kids.

When you see monitoring signals, you need to put an end to the behavior. This is particularly true if the shaming is coming from the most popular kids or the leaders of the class. They are honing a particularly harmful form of leadership. You need to speak to them about this.

Kids may claim they don't know what they're doing; but that's not entirely true. They'll know it's provoking when other kids do it to them. They may not have words for it, so you'll need to articulate expectations. Put a stop to it.

Shaming in the Classroom

Shaming signals will ruin the learning atmosphere of your class. We've all seen this: a child gets up to read aloud, and other kids smirk. He flinches, turns red, and loses his focus. The other kids snicker. Whatever that child was trying to do now becomes impossible. His adrenaline spikes; he starts flooding. The words swim before his eyes. He starts stammering or can't get the words out.

That child is flooding. He feels like a fool. Trapped in front of the classroom, there's no way out.

This child will come to hate standing up in class. You're the leader, and this is your territory. You need to maintain safe space for everyone. It's your job to put an end to shows of contempt.

Don't You Start

Now let's talk about *your* monitoring behaviors. There's going to be a time when you're exasperated, tired, or just fed up. You can't say what's really on your mind, so perhaps you roll your eyes or get a tight smirk on your face. It's tempting to say with body language what you would never say out loud.

If you have something corrective to say, then say it. If you're merely in a bad mood, don't take it out on the kids. Shaming signals are off-limits.

Signals of contempt can get an explosive reaction, and kids are particularly vulnerable to responding in this way. You want to model a higher brand of leadership.

One Exception: No Fool

There is one exception where it is all right to give in and roll your eyes. That is when a child is willfully trying to provoke you and play you for a fool. In situations like this, it's clear you aren't showing contempt for the child. You're showing that you're wildly unimpressed by the ploy.

For instance, one teacher was at her limit with a 9-year-old boy we'll call Eldridge. She had a time-out corner in the room, marked off with yellow tape. She not only put Eldridge inside the box, she called in a security guard to stand over Eldridge and make sure he stayed in the box.

All right, this teacher was overreacting. Eldridge was showing that he could game adults.

Eldridge looked sideways up at the security guard and wiggled one foot so his toes touched the yellow line. Then he wiggled his toes just over the line. And then Eldridge looked up at the guard again.

The security guard, a big, burly man who naturally lived in authority posture, just rolled his eyes, as if to say, "You cannot believe I'd be fool enough to fall for that."

Eldridge clearly needed an adult he couldn't game. He got attention by making fools of adults. The security guard was wildly unimpressed, and Eldridge found someone to relate to.

When a kid is actively gaming you, a good-natured eye roll is not a bad response. It can say you know what they're up to, you're in on the ploy, and there's no way you're going to take the bait.

Summing It Up:
High Points of Chapter Three

Understanding body language is essential to managing a class or intervening around aggression. It provides a way to spot fights as they're brewing, and it helps you act *before* things get out of control. A command of good body language is essential to help you be the best teacher you can be.

For Teachers

Flooding interferes with verbal communication.

Body language is the back-up plan if words fail. And words will fail, often.

If you grew up with social media, you may have less experience reading body language and social cues.

Leadership signals include upright posture, a five-point direct stance, direct gaze, and a low, resonant voice. These are the signals you want.

Smile with your eyes.

Say nothing when you're furious. You'll have fewer regrets, and properly used, silence is more effective than words.

People using authority signals are assumed to be intelligent, trustworthy, and worthy of being followed.

Belligerence signals include a "charging bull" posture, a snarling voice, a jutting jaw, clenched fists, and pounding on the desk. The belligerent adult wants to be in charge but is really out of control. Belligerence escalates aggression.

Belligerence spikes adrenaline; these signals will actually inhibit your students' learning.

Submissive Signals

Submissive signs include hunched posture, diminished stance, fidgeting, evasive or distracted eyes, and a high or breathy voice.

Submissive signals undermine your authority, invite your class to disregard you, and make classroom management all but impossible.

Shaming signals include rolling the eyes, smirking, mocking humor, disapproving cough, exasperated sniff. Shaming is powerful and damaging.

Submissive students may be perceived as dishonest, weak, liars, "losers" and none too bright. None of this may be true.

Model and teach leadership signals, including authoritative body language while showing students how to present or how to read out loud.

Mixed messages may mask fear. Tread carefully; this can be explosive. Avoid words like *scared* or *afraid*. Instead, use terms like *under pressure, stressed,* or *overloaded.*

When a child is gaming you, good-natured monitoring behaviors can be OK. It's as if to say, "You surely can't believe I'd fall for that."

For Students

Belligerent signals are a sign that a fight is brewing. Use this information to head off fights before they happen.

Teachers may perceive students with belligerence signals as disruptive, defiant, and overall, trouble. This may not necessarily be the case; belligerent students may simply be angry about unrelated things and not know how to deal with their feelings.

Students showing submissive signals often get bullied by other children. Spend time with them to make sure they know they're appreciated and welcome. Check to see if they're being bullied.

Chapter Four

Escalation and De-escalation

A t this point, we can look at how both adrenaline and body language play into escalation. And we can use all the skills gained up to now to de-escalate situations.

Teachers who are good at de-escalation have some consistent traits:

They stay relatively calm. They don't flood as much as other people; they remain relatively clear-headed while dealing with situations. They're not easily angered or upset.

They're good at "reading" situations. They can quickly and accurately gauge what's going on. Even when things are chaotic and loud, they have a sense for what's serious and what's not and what's needed at the moment.

Most people see a fight as a blur and view escalation through a fog of alarm. They don't take in information well. They tend to magnify what they do see, often overreacting. Viewing things through their own fear, they miss significant signals, including signs the kid has just done something right. In contrast, teachers who are good at de-escalation see the things most people miss.

They see kids acting out as human. They don't demonize. An aggressive student makes sense to them in some way; he's not a tornado, a force of nature, or a defiant little brat. Since these teachers can see the complete human being inside the aggressive student, they're more successful at reaching him.

CIT Model

In this chapter, we'll explore a de-escalation model originally developed for Crisis Intervention Teams (CITs) on mental health calls. The CIT movement started in Memphis in 1988 after police were called to a mental health crisis and the situation spun out of control. The mentally ill person was killed.

The community as a whole decided there must be a better way. The mental health community, police, counselors, and families all came together to work out a new approach to handling volatile situations. This de-escalation model is just part of the outcome.

I first learned this model from the Chicago Police Crisis Intervention Team. You might not think of police as experts in mental health, and they're not. But they're the ones who get called in a crisis, so they needed to have working skills.

Just as mental health is not a teacher's job, it is not a cop's job either. Like a really good teacher, a really good cop is a great judge of human nature. This model offers excellent, practical insights into aggression and how it shifts towards violence.

The Five-Stage Escalation Scale

The five-stage escalation scale says that violence doesn't come out of nowhere. It builds, and it builds in a somewhat predictable way.

The person escalating—say, the student—is on the left. The teacher who intervenes is on the right.

	Student	Teacher
Level 5	Violence	Anger/fear
Level 4	Hostility	Fear
Level 3	Anger	Anxiety
Level 2	Anxiety	Empathy
Level 1	Calm	Supportive

We'll look at the left side first, the kid who's losing control. The baseline starts from a state of calm. Then it escalates first into anxiety, then anger, then hostility, and finally, violence.

All these states, except for calm, involve flooding. Escalation takes the flooding closer and closer to violence.

Let's take a closer tour of the chart.

Calm

The baseline is calm, at least whatever passes for calm for this kid. She may be wired or hyperactive; it may feel like she never stops moving. But if this kid is stable, then that's her level of calm.

Now, a traumatized student may only be calm in her sleep. Most of her waking existence is anxious, angry, or worse. But you need to know what calm looks like for this kid, because that is your target state.

Too often when a normally problematic kid is calm, she promptly gets ignored. For once, she's not causing trouble. Consider the message this sends. If she needs to be acknowledged, the only workable way of accomplishing that is by making trouble for you.

So when this kid is calm—working quietly by herself or cooperating with others—find some way to give positive feedback. If there are only five minutes when this child is calm and displaying positive behaviors, give positive feedback in those five minutes. If the next time she manages six minutes of calm behavior, give positive feedback for that. Reward behavior that goes in the right direction.

But sometimes despite our best efforts behavior escalates.

Anxiety

Adrenaline drives fight or flight, and an anxious child is in flight mode. He may feel threatened or trapped, feel that other people are too close, or feel that he urgently wants to be elsewhere. An anxious kid may stay home from school, pleading a stomachache, or he may cause a situation at school in order to get sent home. An anxious youngster who feels defensive may lash out. But his first choice is to back away or to get you to back off.

Anxiety may present with agitation, fear, or defiance. Typical statements are "Leave me alone!" or "Why do I always have to ___." At the level of anxiety, the child's priority is get space and safety, not to fight you.

This kid needs to be safe from insult, threat, or loss of face. But things can get worse if his anxiety keeps spinning out of control.

Anger

The next stage is anger. An angry person is shifting from flight to fight. Typically angry statements go on the attack: "I hate you." "You're awful." "You don't care. None of you care."

Anger is broad and generic. It's marked by general "you" statements: "You don't care." "You've got it in for me." "You can all go to hell."

Angry children are loud and often rude, but they're burning through their adrenaline. So they may downshift on their own.

Kids often become angry quickly and react impulsively. "Hey, quit shoving!" "I didn't shove you. You shoved me!" In this case, the trajectory is moving in the wrong direction, but we're not in the red zone yet.

Hostility

The next stage is hostility. *Now* we're in the red zone. Hostility is defined as having a specific target, a directed threat, and possessing the means to carry out that threat.

For instance, a teen may say, "You can go to hell," but she does not have the means to carry it out. She cannot send you to hell. Though clearly she would love to, she lacks the authority to make that happen.

But let's say a boy narrows his eyes at another boy and says, "I'm going to get that guy," and then gathers his friends to lie in wait after school. He's got a specific target, a threat directed at someone in particular, and he's acquired the means to carry out his plan. Violence is imminent.

If one kid is saying terrible things but moving backwards toward the door, a fight is not imminent. By moving backward, the child is *removing* the means to carry out the threat. This is just fronting. You can't punch someone from 30 feet away, but you can sure put up a good show.

Hostility—a specific target, a directed threat, and the means to carry out the threat—is the last stop before violence. At this point you'll need to act decisively because you won't like where it goes next.

Violence

Violence is the fifth stage of the escalation cycle. By this I don't mean a snowball fight or a shoving match, but a genuine effort to hurt someone.

You can see by re-reading the chart that violence isn't something that just happens without sense or warning. Violence is the last in a series of emotional states. If you head it off early by shifting down to one of the earlier states, you can prevent the outbreak.

Your job is to intervene at an earlier point in the chart—at anxiety, anger, or hostility—because you are not about to let it get to violence.

Reading Situations

Here are some verbal flags that will help you gauge the stages of escalation:

Calm people tend to talk about the situation at hand, playing with a truck, socializing, whatever.

Anxious people suddenly start talking about themselves, using words like *I, me,* and *my*: "I'm from New York and nobody talks to *me* that way." The translation is, "I'm anxious because nobody else is from New York, and it doesn't count for anything around here."

Angry people talk in generalities with a generic you, as in, "You teachers! Like you care." or "You're always telling me what to do!"

Hostile people, moving toward violence, draw a tight focus, a pinpoint target. They use the word "you" precisely now, or they wordlessly zero in as the rest of the world disappears.

This is how escalation might look with a young boy playing with a truck:

"Vroom! Climb up, higher. Over the top!" (Talking about the truck: Calm.)

"Mine! It's *my* truck." (Talking about himself: Anxiety.)

"You get away. You're stupid!" (Using the generic *you* and general aggression: Anger.)

Without saying a word, he goes to a tight focus, jaw jutting, fists clenched. A fight is imminent. (Precise target, directed threat, and the means to carry out the threat: Hostility.)

This is how escalation looks with a preteen girl:

"Abraham Lincoln? What chapter was that?" (Talking about task: Calm.)

"Why do I have to read about Abraham Lincoln? What's that ever going to mean to me?" (Talking about herself: Anxiety.)

Or the favorite:

"I don't have to listen to you. My father's a lawyer!" (Talking about herself: Anxiety.)

"What do you know? What makes you think you're so smart?" (Generic *you*, general insult: Anger.)

She gets up, with a charging bull posture and clenched fists, slams down her books, and glares at her opponent like there's no one else in the world. (Precise target, directed threat, and the means to carry out the threat: Hostility)

Now, with adolescence, kids talk about themselves constantly (also tweet about themselves, take pictures of themselves, text about themselves, etc.!). They're socially anxious and can stay that way for years.

You may notice that a kid who is good, say, in math, can lose himself in the task. His anxiety falls away. He feels secure enough to be busy with things other than himself.

Calm is actually a gift of computers. Computers are so compelling that they allow kids to forget about themselves and their anxieties and focus on the task at hand. The computer isn't scary, like adults. And the more they master the technical world, the more they want to interact with it.

This is in contrast to some adults, who feel anxious around computers. Because they feel anxious and insecure, they avoid the computer as much as the third-grader avoids social studies.

Intervention

According to the chart, violence isn't something that just happens, like spontaneous combustion. Violence is the last in a series of emotional states.

The earlier you intervene, the easier a situation is to manage. Calm is the target state, where your students function best and learn. By the time they hit anxiety, trouble's brewing. It may not be a problem at the moment, but it could well be a problem shortly. If things have gone to anger, the trajectory is going in the wrong direction. You need to reverse the trend. By hostility, you have got to kick into action. The window of opportunity is closing.

Anxiety is easier to de-escalate than anger, and anger is easier to de-escalate than hostility. Your best opportunities are further down the scale.

For instance, it's nearly impossible to intervene during a full blown tantrum. You know from past experience that if a child is over-tired, stressed, or anxious, he will probably get short-tempered. The edginess builds, and you can see the tantrum coming on. You can spot the escalation in process. If you get the child a cup of juice, put him down for a nap, or provide some quiet time, you can head off the tantrum. You step the child back down the chart.

Protocols

Escalation goes from calm to anxiety, then to anger and hostility; de-escalation moves in the opposite direction. We spot where students are on the chart, then step them down one level: If they are hostile, we step them down to anger, where they can burn off their feelings harmlessly. If they are angry, we step them down to anxiety. And if we catch them at anxiety, our job is to bring them back to calm.

Authoritative body language, including that low voice of authority, works extremely well at de-escalating children. Keep a calm, steady expression on your face. Your voice is firm, but kind. Strong, reassuring body language is especially good with anxious children. Remember, body language gets through when words fail.

Since the student may be feeling trapped, take a step backward. Give the student room to breathe; remember, flooding people have a greater need for space, and flooding magnifies. If a child is very anxious, move so you're not between the child and the door. It's not necessarily that they're going anywhere, but they may feel less trapped if you move.

If there's a threat to the child's ego, back off the threat. You might say something like, "Actually, Howard, I think you're very smart. And I think you can do a lot better than this."

You'll know if these are the right words, because you'll see a sudden shift.

The anxious kid wants safety, and you just signaled that he's safe. He may look at you like this is too much to hope for. Go easy. You don't want to say a lot of silly stuff that isn't true. You just need to be clear that he's respected and safe in your territory. Move him toward calm.

Adults on the Chart

Now that we can make sense of the child who's escalating, let's look at the other side of the chart: us. Remember, the upset child isn't the only one caught on the escalation scale. The teacher or administrator can get caught up as well.

This was a crucial discovery of the original researchers: There is interplay in escalation. The more the child loses stability, the more it upsets the adult. And as the adult loses stability, she can unknowingly make things worse.

The base level starts with the calm child. At that level, it's easy for a teacher to be supportive: calm student, supportive adult. That describes school on a good day. But of course, it's not always a good day.

If the child shifts to anxiety, the teacher still has patience to attend. Let's say the child freezes up in class. Well, the adult may show empathy or understanding. It's relatively easy to be empathetic and sympathetic to a child who's worried or anxious.

It's harder when the anxiety is masked by bravado or a tough exterior, which becomes more common by middle school. But once you sense the child is secretly scared, it's easier to be sympathetic.

The next stage from the child is anger. Anger is more threatening. The teacher or administrator stops feeling empathetic and shifts to anxiety, feeling the need to bring this under control.

If the child escalates to hostility, the adult moves from anxiety to fear. And if the child crosses to violence, the adult responds with either fear or outright anger.

This escalation chart is highly interactive. As the student gets increasingly aggressive and less stable, the adult gets increasingly upset and less stable. And that becomes a formula for trouble.

De-escalation

The escalation chart also works in the opposite direction. By taking control of our own reaction, we can lead students down the scale. By keeping ourselves calm, we can help the child calm down. By catching our own anxiety and deliberately stepping down, we can get the upset kid to come with us.

Think of the teachers you know who are most effective at de-escalating situations. They seem to have an inner coolness. They rarely look out of control. If they are feeling worried, great body language masks it.

In a situation that's escalating, the first thing to keep in mind is similar to flooding: Watch your own reaction. Calm down. You have to have control of yourself before you can control your students.

This is counterintuitive. When students start escalating, the natural thing is to get angry and start shouting. But when you do that, you have spiked their adrenaline and have just jumped up the scale.

You may think you're taking control. In fact, you've just demonstrated that you're out of control.

Real World

In some ways this chart is idealistic. It presumes, for example, that if the child is calm, the adult is supportive, and that if the child is anxious, the adult is empathetic. That's a reasonable assumption; what is a teacher's role, if not to be supportive? But real life isn't always that way.

We can arrive at school and find calm children, but we've been stuck in traffic for half an hour. Or we might have started fighting during breakfast with the spouse and come into work to find a nasty note in our mailbox. We're not calm; we're irritated. Our students quickly sense our irritation and become anxious. Once anxious, they act out— because they're kids after all—and they may not know what to do with anxiety beyond squabble and punch each other.

You'll notice that the days when you are really stressed are the days when the kids act out. Actually, the kids absorb our stress and echo it back at us. So really, they're not pushing us up the escalation scale; we're pushing them.

Escalation and Control

When working with staff in psychiatric units, Zak and I noticed a curious pattern. Sometimes the most meticulous, organized nurses sparked the most escalation.

These nurses were highly professional. They did things by the book. But they worked in psychiatric units, so something was always going wrong. Someone was always spilling their juice, losing their meds, or saying the wrong thing. And this happened every day.

The same exacting, perfectionist skills that helped them thrive in college left them exasperated in a psychiatric setting.

Of course similar problems turn up in the classroom. The teachers with the strongest need to have things "right" are often most easily irritated and angered. When things weren't right—as was so often the case—they quickly moved up the escalation scale, ahead of the kids.

Sometimes teachers or administrators believe that the answer is to "toughen the kid up." If the child looks anxious—read "weak"—the adult will come down hard. If the child has a background of trauma and is acting out, the adult may come down harder because "It's a tough world out there."

It *is* a tough world out there. But based on what we know about adrenaline and trauma, this is precisely the wrong way to prepare the child to be resilient in the face of that toughness. The kids aren't getting tougher; they're getting bitter and, often, more out of control.

In the next example we'll look at a story where adults did not do well on their side of the chart. We'll follow that with a story where adults seized the opportunity to help students de-escalate.

Missed Opportunity

This is the case of a 14-year-old girl we'll call Jo, who was in a school that only went up to eighth grade. She was not the kind of obedient girl that adults find easy to like. The school was in an underprivileged district where the principal believed in being tough on the kids so they could face a tough world.

Jo had a great deal of trauma in her immediate background. She had recently been sexually assaulted, and her home had been torched, with her in it by a neighbor. As we know, trauma makes kids volatile and alienated from adults. Jo conformed to this pattern.

In her favor, Jo was a smart kid who wanted to be in school and who really wished to learn. But raw nerves and volatility meant she got in continual confrontations with teachers and security guards.

Jo was sexually developed for her age and sexually active, which upset the teachers. They thought she should no longer be in that school. She made teachers uncomfortable and often angry. After confrontations, Jo would disappear for a while. By the time she came back, teachers would be angry about her missing school, and the cycle would start all over again.

Jo wasn't in a gang, so the tough girls didn't like her. The good kids didn't like her. Only one of the teachers liked her, so she would shelter with that teacher, finding excuses to be in her room.

The continual cycle of provocations meant school just wasn't working. The teacher knew that other teachers wanted Jo out of their classrooms, so she hunted for computer-based ways the kid could do schoolwork away from people.

At the same time, Jo was having chronic conflicts with a female security guard, who would make openly disparaging remarks about Jo's clothes and physical development. The girl would respond, "Why are you talking to me this way? You're a grown-up. You have no right to talk to me that way."

Finally, Jo got into a confrontation with a large male security guard who hauled her into a small, closed interrogation room. Well, we know the effects of flooding, and they are magnified in enclosed spaces.

The guard kept bellowing, "You are being disrespectful!" He was in full, thundering belligerence. Jo was so upset she started clawing her own arms. The guard was so angry he seemed to take the clawing as another form of disobedience, so he kept shouting louder.

Someone fetched the teacher, who walked in and turned on the guard: "You do NOT speak to this girl this way. Stop yelling!" The guard stormed out.

The teacher tried to calm down Jo, but the guard went to the principal and reported the teacher for disrespecting him. So before the teacher could get Jo out of the room, the principal stormed in and yelled at the teacher for undermining school discipline.

Jo did not come back after that. She disappeared completely.

If security guards are supposed to keep the peace, this wasn't working. Let's look at some of the missed opportunities for helping Jo before we look at a better plan.

Safe Space

Jo sought refuge in the teacher's room. It was someplace she could be without confrontation.

Beleaguered kids will seek out safe spaces and retreat there: a teacher who listens, science club, or the back of the room feeding goldfish. They are seeking calm, a place to stabilize. Remember, on the escalation chart, calm is the goal. Cut off their retreat and you escalate the fight.

Now, this doesn't mean the kids get everything their way. It's fair to bargain for the retreat: "If you do X, you get to feed the iguana." But if feeding the iguana brings calm, your goal includes the child feeding the iguana until you find the next source of calm.

The teacher tried to expand the safe space by letting Jo do her work alone on a computer. This was actually a good plan, but everything blew up before they were able to implement it.

In volatile situations, technology can create a buffer zone. Adults and kids can readily set each other off, but computers are much more neutral. Yes, kids need to develop human skills, but when necessary, computer time can help students stabilize.

As it was, other teachers and security guards did not see safe space as positive. They thought this teacher was coddling the girl. The situation only got worse, in the interrogation room when the sympathetic teacher intervened.

One way to create safe space—and get escalated adults to accept it—is to give the child a job. It does not matter what the child is doing: washing lab equipment, hauling gym gear, running math programs, or helping little kids. Virtually anything will do, as long as it looks like she's working.

Saving Face

The teacher in Jo's story—who meant well—made a serious mistake. She went into that small room and yelled at the security guard who was yelling at the girl. He was in anger, she was in anger, and the girl was in panic. They did not need any more flooding in that small room.

Having been yelled at and thrown out of the room, the guard also needed to save face. Be realistic: many adults will escalate off the chart if they feel they've lost face.

If the teacher did not allow the guard to save face, he would surely get his revenge. And he did.

It goes back to that reoccurring question: Would you rather be right or be effective? The teacher may have been right, but if she wanted to be effective, she needed to get the guard out of the room while allowing him to save face. It could have been as simple as, "Thank you, Mr. Howard. Could you step outside with me a moment?" She had two parties to de-escalate, and she only addressed one.

Justice

Sometimes a child may lay claim to justice. For instance, Jo insisted that the first security guard was an adult and should not comment about her body. She was making a claim for justice.

Jo had recently been sexually assaulted, and someone had burned down her house. Nearly everyone in her school despised her. What would she know about justice? Yet she felt the need for it keenly.

But the appeal to justice is a hit-or-miss skill. If the child somehow gets through, and if the adult reconsiders, things may improve. But this doesn't often happen. If, as in Jo's case, an appeal to justice is seen as defiance, it can bring anger, escalation, and disaster.

Kids can rarely gauge whether they are getting through. It's a shot in the dark. You can sometimes see them feeling their way, speaking from the heart, although still flooding.

Kids often employ de-escalation skills, but they're haphazard. Their skills are imperfect; sometimes they work and sometimes they backfire. But pay attention to the skill set. The kid is trying. You need to help her improve her skills.

Opportunity: Security and De-escalation

The following example has many similar elements: rough conditions, inappropriate security guards, and students taking the brunt of adult behavior. But in this, case things were turned around. Adults worked with the kids' need for justice and made an appreciable improvement.

The Chicago Public School system (CPS) wanted to lower violence rates in the schools but had been getting complaints about security guards. The issues were similar to those in the last story: Guards were escalating situations, making inappropriate comments, and behaving as if they didn't like students at all.

The CPS surveyed the students to get a better sense of the situation. The first surprise was that the students, overall, were reasonable in their assessments. They understood that security was hard, and they didn't want or expect guards to be "too chummy." Students wanted the guards to be authorities. But they also wanted the security guards to be fair, to be reasonable, and to model the same conflict resolution skills they urged on the kids. Students also knew very well who was a good guard and who wasn't.

The kids wanted guards at the front door—the first adults they see in the morning—to smile and act like they were glad students were there. They wanted guards to be proactive, de-escalating situations before things got out of hand. If guards did have to intervene, kids wanted it to be a learning experience, not just brute force.

Students also reported guards who made comments about students' bodies, and they absolutely wanted that to stop.

Jadine Chou, who commissioned the survey, then had some of the teens tape videos where they talked directly to the guards about incidents that had happened to them. These students were speaking to justice. They talked about what had happened, how it had affected them, and how they wished the guards had handled things.

This was a dramatic change for students and security alike. Students had never been asked what they thought before or been asked what they needed from adults who intervened.

The guards listened to the kids on video, and the great majority of guards responded to the training. Kids on tape weren't threatening the way kids in front of them might be. A few guards weren't interested in changing; they resigned or were fired. One who was noted for making sexual comments didn't return, no explanation.

When interviewed again a year after this training, students noted a marked improvement in guard behavior; they said sometimes the guards even smiled or acted more human. For instance, if a student was crying in the hallway, a guard would now ask what was wrong rather than barking at her to get to class.

It also resulted in a marked drop in violence. Serious incidents, such as battery, were down 15%. In-school arrests were down 25%.

If your school wants to achieve a similar success, this approach would not be hard to do. You could use an online survey and smart phone videos, none of which are very expensive.

This story has many parallels to the original de-escalation study from Memphis: Ask people what they need in order to calm down. Their requirements may be surprisingly reasonable. Make sure professionals know how to de-escalate situations, rather than inadvertently making things worse. Model good behavior. Increase calm.

These are reasonable, "doable" tasks. Apart from using de-escalation skills, the adults needed to manage their own flooding and be aware of their body language.

It is also worth noting the difference it made when the guards began to act like they wanted students there. We do not want vulnerable kids to drop out. If we want them to stay in school, we need to show them that we want them in the building.

Making kids feel welcome means no monitoring behaviors: no rolling our eyes at the kids or making belittling comments. If we owned a store, we'd never expect a customer to come back after being treated with monitoring behaviors. In fact, shaming behaviors drive people away. We need to do better with kids.

Bad Kids

One of the behaviors we see in teachers who are gifted at de-escalation is that they don't demonize kids. They see the person within, and they can reach that person. But there's a reason some teachers easily relate to troubled kids.

Most teachers are former good kids. Having thrived in school, it's natural to return there for a career.

But in many schools, there's a hidden resource: former bad kids. And these former bad kids can be surprisingly good at reaching kids with behavior problems. Having once been bad kids themselves, they see today's bad kids in a different light.

Teachers who were formerly bad kids usually keep their background hidden. So many of my best interviewees said to me, "You're not going to bust me, are you? Nobody knows this about me. You're not going to tell everyone are you?"

I won't give away their secrets. But these grown, former "bad kids" now working in schools see kids through a different lens. They find unexpected solutions. They're a valuable resource, and they need to be heard.

Typically, they're careful in what they say. They may offer insights but omit why they know or where they happened to see that behavior before. Being careful, they say less than they know.

It's in everyone's interest to make the most of this wisdom. But bear in mind, if the former bad kids are going to step forward, they need cooperation and protection. One reported that she *did* step forward to talk about her past, and a smug colleague used it against her at every opportunity.

The other unusually insightful group is made up of teachers who had bad kids as relatives. They watched their brother or sister act out. They also got to know, firsthand, what worked and what didn't.

So if you have doubts about sharing your personal insights as a former "bad kid," put the stories on your brothers or cousins. Ruin their reputations; hopefully, they live in another town. But get the stories out there. Your colleagues need you, and they need your stories.

Summing It Up:
High Points of Chapter Four

People don't just explode; they escalate in a roughly orderly fashion. We can use this knowledge to read a situation, gauging whether things are getting calmer or more volatile, and to intervene before violence takes place.

The five stages of escalation are calm, anxiety, anger, hostility, and violence.

Adults who intervene escalate too. When kids are calm, adults tend to be supportive; when kids are anxious, adults tend to be empathetic. As kids shift to anger, adults get anxious; by the time kids get hostile, adults become fearful. By the time kids reach violence, the intervening adults tend to be either angry or fearful.

You can help take control of the situation by managing your own reactions.

It is easier to intervene at the lower stages. This is your best window of opportunity.

At hostility, violence is imminent. The window of opportunity is closing. This is the time for immediate action.

Verbal flags: While calm, kids tend to talk about the subject at hand. At anxiety, they talk about themselves (*I* or *my*). At anger they use the word *you* in the general sense. At hostility they adopt an intense, laser focus, using the word *you* very specifically.

Kids have de-escalation skills, which are often overlooked. These skills may be flawed or still developing, but this is fertile ground. Work with it.

Kid skills include: seeking a safe space, making an appeal to justice, or submerging themselves in technology. Kids sometimes also have an intuitive sense for saving face.

Computers and technology can serve as a buffer between kids and angry adults.

If you cut off a kid's retreat to a safe space you escalate a conflict.

continued ...

Losing face will cause many adults to escalate. Allow flooding adults to save face by politely asking them to step away with you, using a calm authority posture, and saying "Please" and "Thank you." This is not the time to lose your temper.

Toughening kids up, when trauma is at the root of their behavior, does not make kids more prepared for life. It tends to make them bitter and more out of control.

It is inappropriate for an adult to comment on a youngster's body, appearance, or sexuality. Enforce the dress code, but otherwise keep all comments to yourself.

Adults need to model the same de-escalation skills they want to build in students.

A brief survey and videotaped statements from students can be an inexpensive and powerful force for change.

Ask volatile kids what they need in order to calm down. Their requirements may be surprisingly reasonable.

Former "bad kids" who work in schools are a hidden resource; they can be surprisingly good at reaching kids with behavioral problems.

CHAPTER FIVE

Grades K-2: The Safe Foundation

A t this point we'll take a break from high conflict and focus instead on calm. The importance of calm can't be overemphasized. It's not enough to keep managing crises. Calm is a worthwhile goal, even though at times it may seem difficult to reach. A safe and calm learning environment is the right of every child.

Kindergarten through second grade sets the foundation for a child's future in school and perhaps in life. It also sets a foundation for behavior. Behavior problems at this stage can result in a child never learning to learn; one child's behavior can even prevent the entire class from learning effectively, as the teacher struggles to keep order.

In establishing a calm, safe classroom, we'll apply many of the principles we've covered so far, including reducing flooding, enhancing calm, and reducing anxiety before it builds to anger. We also want to establish safe, calm habits and head off negative behaviors before they take root.

In setting this safe foundation, we'll emphasize skills that will benefit children for the rest of their lives. These include self-regulation, dealing with rules, and social skills, such as working well with others and positive leadership.

These aren't just student goals. We want students and parents pulling together as a team, rather than operating at cross-purposes. Of course there will always be exceptions, kids who resist a calm pattern, but then you're dealing with two or three behavior problems, rather than twenty-five.

While much of this chapter is best suited for early grades, some elements can be adapted for older children. If you teach a higher grade, look over this chapter and see if any of these techniques could help in your classroom.

Remember: if you have to enforce constant discipline, there will not be much time left to teach. If kids learn to work as a team, they can get along without your constant reprimands. Peer pressure can be a powerful force. You want it working for you, rather than against you.

Establishing a Safe, Calm Classroom

The first step is to create a safe and calm classroom. Chaos breeds anxiety, and we know where that goes. It is easier to keep anxiety to a minimum than it is to perform damage control after things have escalated.

And it isn't just the students who do better in a calm classroom. A smoothly working classroom will leave the teacher less stressed, with a clearer head and more emotional resources to handle the issues that *do* arise.

This chapter follows a number of the guidelines set down by Harry and Rosemary Wong in their book *Your First Days of School*. Judy Planthe, a wise teacher and mentor, introduced me to this approach, which has been used for years by a network of master teachers. Their students ranged from poor to wealthy; they swore by this cooperative system.

A Strong Foundation

The Wongs state that the primary problem with out of control classrooms isn't discipline at all. Rather, it's the lack of procedures and routines. If you start by introducing solid expectations in a simple framework, you can avoid the great majority of behavior problems. A few kids may still act out, but those are the exceptions.

This approach requires a little investment in time to set up the system. However, it more than pays off in the discipline problems you'll avoid later.

Order

Order wards off discipline problems, but this is not about ruling with an iron fist. It's about setting up clear protocols that make sense. This way children know what's expected of them, and it feels natural to go along with the rules.

We are social creatures. We take cues from each other on what's acceptable and what's not. Children take cues from teachers, parents, and each other. You want everyone traveling in the right direction.

In the early years, when kids first arrive at school, everything is new and uncertain. This creates anxiety until they know what to expect. Routines and clear expectations give them the comfort and security necessary to settle into a predictable world.

Anxiety can manifest in constant questions and interruptions that can try your patience: "Miss, when do we get our snack?" "Miss, can

I sharpen my pencil now?" Students' constant tugging is a result of anxiety. Once kids know the procedures and routines, there will be less disruption.

The easiest way to lower that anxiety is to introduce your system from the first day, in a friendly, sensible way. The lessons start as they walk in the door. Introduce them to the basics: where to sit, where to hang their coat, when snack time is, and when lunch time is. The children will also need to be shown where the closest bathroom is and how you expect them to let you know they've left the room.

Some teachers have a board with the kids' names on a magnet. One side is labeled "In the Room," and the other labeled "Out of the Room." Kids move their magnet to the "Out of the Room" side if they have to be excused and move it back to the "In the Room" side when they return. A good rule is to have no more than two children out of the room at once, or you may find your students off disrupting some other part of the school.

At the beginning of the year, the children are in a new environment that doesn't yet make sense. Anxiety centers in a part of the brain that's very concrete, so you need to cover concrete needs first.

Next, cover *when* things happen. Post the day's schedule on the chalkboard. If they don't yet know how to read or tell time, you can use symbols, say, for reading or math. Even if they can't tell time, they can see that daily activities follow a sequence. They'll know where they are in the day, and how long it is until their next snack. And a posted schedule is not a bad incentive to help them learn to read time, so they can see for themselves.

Go over the schedule for the day. This is particularly important if there's anything unusual: "At 10:30 this morning there will be an assembly." This way the children won't keep asking, "What's going on? What are we doing next?"

On many days the schedule will be fixed and predictable: music on Monday, gym on Thursday, and so on. Stability and the repetition of the schedule help them get used to the way things are.

Kids get insecure if they don't know what's coming. You get pelted with questions: "How are we going to...?" "Are you going to help us?" The anxiety might be particularly pronounced for kids with any sort of learning disability or autism. Children on the autistic spectrum often need their own personal agenda right at their desk.

This system is not unlike the concrete order of boot camp in the military. It offers stability in a strange environment, helps clarify expectations, and brings stability and unity to the group.

With procedures in place, if a child forgets and gets agitated, another child might remind her. This is good for both of them: They're developing the skills to handle problems on their own, without getting you involved. This leaves you more precious time for teaching, and helps keep you from getting overloaded.

Class Rules

The Wongs suggest working with the kids to set up their own rules for the classroom. Of course there are rules for the school as a whole: Be safe. Be responsible. Be ready to learn. But the Wongs suggest that each class agree on a short set of rules that will be all their own.

Spend some time talking with the kids: How can we make this school year a good year? Every class will come up with similar basics, like not fighting, being good to each other, or doing their work.

You will probably only need four or five rules. Write your kids' suggestions in a positive way. Then make up a poster with the rules, and have all the kids sign it.

Your class's rules go up on a chart on the wall. It might look something like this:

These are our rules:
We are kind to each other.
We listen to the teacher and to each other.
We complete our work and do our best.
We raise our hands when we want to talk.
We all help clean up.

This not only provides a clear sense of order and expectation, but talking about the rules and having your students sign the poster also gets you buy-in from your students. They all discuss the rules, and they all sign. If, later, one kid starts acting out, another kid might remind her of what was agreed to.

Getting Parents on Board

At the start of the year, you also want to get the parents on board. You and the parents are allies, and you'll need to work together as a team. So open the door to the parents.

An excellent idea from Virginia Brucker is to send out a welcome to parents before the school year. Have a set of questions for parents to fill out:

What do I need to know about your child?
Tell me about your child's strengths and concerns.
What are your goals for the year?
What kinds of things does your child do in his or her spare time?

For example, Harry's parents reported that he was interested in robots and was terrified of storms. So when the teacher needed to get through to Harry, the teacher knew some things that would get his attention.

You don't want your first contact with parents to be all about problems with their child. That only puts parents on defensive. They may bridle at the hint of criticism, thinking: "That person doesn't even know who my kid is."

The more you know about the child, the better you can bridge. And if later you do have to go to the parent with a concern, you've already established a friendly footing.

Another possibility is to have a meet-the-teacher or parent-orientation night. This becomes your time to meet parents and outline your expectations for your students. Be sure to bring up classroom rules, so the parents are on board.

In the same meeting you can explain ways to help with homework. This can save all the adults a world of trouble. A new teacher may want to work with a more experienced colleague who teaches a similar grade level to prepare for parent orientation. They could prepare their meet-the-teacher night talk together, or they could team-teach by each giving half of the presentation.

Focus

Children need to focus in order to do their work. Often focus has to be learned. If they can't hold focus long enough to get work done, they're bound to get into trouble.

In the early years, the key is to keep assignments short and concrete and reinforce students' progress in concrete ways. The Wongs suggest each day giving each child an index card with his or her name and the date. As they successfully complete tasks, they get a sticker on their card.

Let's say you hand out a single sheet for a reading assignment. If the children are able to read it in a reasonable time, they get a sticker on their card. Strong readers might be asked to read more, while struggling readers are asked to read only one section.

Now, some educators do not believe in using stickers as rewards, suggesting that this essentially amounts to bribing children to learn. If you are uncomfortable with stickers, a different approach might be to have a set of easily personalized notes, such as: "___ had a great day today because ___."

This gives you a different way to provide personalized, positive reinforcement without the appearance of bribes. Other teachers have other favorite methods to reinforce desired behavior. Whatever your classroom philosophy, you want to provide clear guidance and keep parents in the loop.

If the child is working slowly or has trouble focusing, you can put a timer next to her. This becomes a game: if the child beats the timer, she gets a sticker, a note, or another sign of success. Kids like to beat the timer. Give the child enough time to complete the task and get the reward.

Reading is just an example here. The focus that's developed in reading will carry over to math or any other sort of schoolwork. The idea is to learn focus itself.

It's wise to model focus. For instance, you can talk about yourself as if you were an on-task student. Talk through what you'd do: "I have the supplies I need to do my work. I put my toys away in my backpack so they don't distract me. I won't talk to my friend right now. I'll wait until break time to chat."

If you are using a card with stickers, the card goes home with the child. You may write a brief note, such as "Jackson did a great job completing his math page today." The parent signs the note and sends it back. This way the parents stay in the loop, and the child knows the parent has seen this. It's a visible reminder that the adults are on the same page.

Some schools keep track of daily progress electronically and send weekly emails to parents. The overall effect is the same, keeping parents involved. To keep parents working with you as a team, avoid unpleasant surprises.

Rewards

Reward positive behavior and encourage parents to provide a reward at the end of the week. The most powerful reward is that mom or dad will spend time with the child doing something enjoyable.

Especially if a child has behavior issues, time alone with the parent is a more effective and healthier reward than an object, such as a toy. By encouraging this kind of reward, you actually do more than just keep the parent in the loop. You also teach or remind the parent that the child gets attention after good behavior. A reward might be to go out together and have ice cream, play ball, or whatever the child likes to do.

Parental attention can be an especially important reward in a family where the child hasn't been getting enough attention or attention is given primarily for negative behavior. A child who is desperate for attention learns quickly that negative behavior gets attention. Combine that with the fact that a lot of parents are overwhelmed these days. They may be a single parent, working two jobs, have several children needing their time, or have another child with special needs. Parents may have a hundred distractions. It's entirely possible that the parent may not be aware that the child isn't getting enough attention or is only getting attention for bad behavior. The card system paired with the reward of attention at home gets and keeps the parent continually on the team.

Motivation

All rewards aren't created equal. You need to know which rewards matter to a particular child, and for that you need to know the child.

A toy, or any object, may not be the best motivation. The basic problem may be that the kid has too many toys or is spending too much time with computer games. You do not want to reward the child with more of a bad thing.

Instead, get to know the child's interests. Now, young children may not be able to articulate what really matters to them. Watch the child's face. If the child's eyes light up at the mention of a particular thing or activity, you've found a promising reward.

For instance, one child, Katy, was a special ed student who had difficulty writing. Writing was stressful, so naturally that was when she would act out, talk, or poke other kids.

Katy might have hated writing, but she loved horses; she knew everything about horses. To motivate her and get her to write, the teacher would offer a deal: If she would write five sentences, she could have computer time to look up horses.

Katy was a difficult kid, but this worked for her. She was still stressed, so she'd write quickly. But nonetheless, she was writing. And the more she wrote, the less stressful it was. Meanwhile, she could focus on horses to get her through the writing.

Sometimes the most meaningful reward is free time. In that case, the deal might be: "If you can complete this, you can have eight minutes of free time." Then the child can do whatever he chooses: read a book, play on the computer, color, whatever.

Notice these are not large blocks of time. A large chunk of free time could be a problem, an invitation to get into trouble. But a small block is a burst of pleasure.

A reward is a little like dessert. The first bite is a burst of flavor. But after seven or eight bites, the taste buds don't respond as much. It's the first one that's most intense.

You can take the same approach for a whole class reward. Then kids encourage other kids: "C'mon. Get going, so we can get our free time."

One teacher keeps a big glass jar on her desk. When the majority of the class was quiet, or on task, or whatever behavior she wanted to encourage, she'd drop a marble in the jar. When the class reached the magic number of marbles, the whole class would have ten minutes of free time or time on the playground. She and the class would decide in advance what the rewards would be. This method helps create group cooperation, and they also got very good at counting marbles.

Some teachers report that kids today seem to lack inner motivation. This may have to do with kids having so little free time or with parents being so busy. If the kids are always in structured play or always being told what to do, they haven't had enough practice making decisions for themselves. Motivation may need to be taught or shown by example.

Bored Kids

Kids arrive at school at various levels. One kid may come in just knowing the alphabet, with a limited vocabulary, while others may come in reading at a higher level.

If you don't challenge the more capable students, you will surely have discipline problems. They'll get bored and start acting out.

You will need to differentiate instruction, which is a challenge. Hopefully there are a couple of kids at the same level, so they can work together as a team while you instruct the others.

You'll want both large-group instruction and small-group instruction. You can also have physical work centers, so that kids move from one activity to another. While they're working together in a group, they can help each other. That way, instead of coming up to you, they talk to each other and work things out.

Be careful of one thing though: If the more capable kids are always separated from the others, you may end up creating divisions, rather than developing teamwork and unity. So mix and match as you team kids together. For instance, you might team kids up according to their learning styles or interests: Everyone who loves trains is in this corner.

The idea is to get kids actively used to working together and teaming up rather than squabbling.

Behavior Issues

The advantage of the Wongs' system is that it gets the majority of students cooperating and working as a team. But, of course, some kids will have difficulty with rules. Others may be more aggressive or act out for different reasons.

In order to work on behavior, you need to have some kind of positive relationship with the child. Go back and re-read the welcome sheet filled out by the parent. If you know that a child needs extra attention, you can use the insights from the parents to strike up a conversation. Acknowledge that child. The better your rapport with the child, the more that child will respond to you.

As the child comes in, you may notice he's wound up. You might take the kid aside and ask, "Would you like to be my helper today?" Give the child a special job.

The job may be as simple as, "I need you to take a note to the office." And the sealed note says, "I needed Al to take a walk." So the secretary will read the note and thank Al, who will usually come back in a calmer state of mind.

Or you might suggest, "Why don't you go to the bathroom and get a drink?" The kid is probably flooding, so give him the opportunity for space and time. Some teachers call this a "walk about," as the Australians say.

If the child is wound up, she might have more trouble holding focus or completing tasks. She needs a little extra attention. So you explain to her, "This is what we're going to be doing today. I want you to do this much, and then I'll check in." The extra bit of adult attention—along with the promise of more attention soon—will help the child stay on task.

You can discuss it with the child: "I'll check back in 10 minutes. I think you can get down to here. What do you think?"

If the child completes the task, add more positive attention. You might put a sticky note on her desk and say, "This is because of good behavior. This is because you got down to work, where you needed to be." Be clear about what you're rewarding and why.

Avoid giving negative attention in public. The worst thing is to say out loud in front of the class, "Johnny, you're talking again!" If you make it an issue in front of everyone, you're asking for trouble.

Instead, you might have a secret signal, just between you and the child, something no one else knows. This not only gives the child special attention, but it takes the correction out of the realm of words. It's calmer to use non-verbals to re-direct the child.

Now, if you praise behavior, you're welcome to do that out loud: "Why look at this! You're getting all this completed." Say it in front of class, so others know that if you complete your work you get praised. Then spread the praise around, as the others catch on and do the same.

Another trick is to compliment the child who is following instructions well, sitting quietly, or keeping his hands to himself. Most young children will see that their classmates' appropriate behavior was noticed and copy the behavior that gets attention.

Self-Regulation: The Office

Self-regulation is another important skill for children to acquire. Everyone has good days and bad days. Some days kids may feel irritable; things won't go their way. The tension can build over the course of the day. When life starts getting to them, giving them a line of retreat can help them reset.

Many teachers designate a separate desk they call The Office. It's in the same classroom but apart from the other desks. Some teachers use a low divider to section off The Office. They still need to see what's happening in that area, but it defines the space a little more.

Explain to the children that if they are having difficulty, not getting work completed, or having trouble with another child, they're free to go to The Office.

Now, this is not a time-out corner. The Office is not discipline. It's a choice, a freedom, a line of retreat when a child is over-stimulated or in need of a break. This gives kids the option of space if they're flooding and distance from the irritation.

For instance, you may be in the middle of working with small groups, when all of a sudden a child gets up and goes to The Office. The child is learning how to spot her own problem as it first arises, with a concrete way to deal with it. She is learning to moderate her own behavior.

Children may use The Office if they know they're having trouble getting a task done on time or if another child is annoying them. We all need a separate place sometimes. The Office teaches self-management and saves you from continually having to intervene.

It's important that there's nothing negative about going to The Office. For instance, adults go to the office. Kids see this every day. If nothing else, they know that grown-ups on TV go to the office. It's a mature, adult thing to do.

You can model going to The Office by talking aloud to the class about it: "I'm feeling like I need a quiet place for a few minutes. I want to finish up a note. So I'm going to The Office."

Working It Out: The Listening Station

Many teachers make use of a listening station, essentially a low-tech tape recorder in a corner of a room. When one kid is upset about another kid, she can go and tell her complaint to the tape recorder instead of interrupting the teacher. Periodically through the day, the teacher can listen to the tape to see if there's anything more to be done. This helps keep interruptions to a minimum.

Next to the tape recorder are five or six cards with suggestions, like "Ask the other child to stop." Or "Move my chair farther away." Any message the child records has to include the action the child will be taking to fix things.

This system is good on many levels. It gives the child a set of choices to solve the problem herself and encourages her to flip through different options to see what would work best. It gives the child an outlet for her feelings and keeps the teacher in the loop, even as the kids work things out among themselves. The teacher comes in after the fact, to see how things have been handled, rather than constantly playing cop. This teaches kids to handle problems themselves, having an adult step in only as needed.

The other rule is that the listening station is not to be used if someone is hurt or bleeding. In case of injury, tell the teacher immediately. Otherwise, choose a card and tell it to the listening station.

Tantrums

It does little good to yell at a child having a tantrum. This child is flooding, and flooding won't allow the child to understand what you are saying. He's so loud that he probably couldn't hear you even if that part of his brain was working. A better protocol is to first get the child to calm down somewhat, and then, after the child is functional again, talk with him about a plan to keep himself from getting so upset.

You want to remove the child from class or, if that's not possible, introduce some physical separation. Remember, flooding is contagious. You don't want to stress the rest of the class or the kid to escalate the situation because he has an audience.

It might be OK to say a few words, but not too much. The child is on overload, and more stimulation won't help. The child isn't especially verbal at that moment anyway. What the child most needs is space to calm down.

You can sometimes kneel close to the child or, if appropriate, put a gentle hand on his shoulder or back. This can help ground the child. Of course, this is only if your district allows contact with a child.

Another option is to distract the child by placing things near him, such as brightly colored pattern blocks, a stuffed animal, or a favorite picture book. This gives him an outward focus. Then move away and leave space. Remember, flooding people tend to have a greater need for space. At this point the child might calm down somewhat, at least a notch or two.

The child could go get a drink of water or take a note to the office. This provides physical space and a directed path. By the time the child comes back, he should have calmed down quite a bit.

If the child is ready to get back into work, get him back into the routine. Then, at a later time, talk to the child about his behavior: "Let's talk about what you did. What made you so upset?" Try to get him talking about it in some way.

Children who are shy might draw a picture showing their feelings. You can then use the picture as a basis for discussion. Remember, the fastest path from violent to nonviolent is to teach a child to talk about emotions. If he can use words to get his emotions out, he won't have to throw things.

As you talk together, listen carefully. Depending on the feedback you hear, you might ask the child about what set things off or talk about how his actions affect others.

You can also ask calm questions: "Can we think of other ways to solve the problem without having the tantrum?"

The goal is to get the child to recognize when the overload is happening and that he's getting too worked up. Next he needs strategies to head it off.

When a child has strategies in mind, you should be able to see a difference. If the child starts to get upset at a later point, remind him of his suggestions for himself. Remember, it's better to have the child control himself than for you to do it.

"Social stories" are another great resource, particularly for special-ed kids with autism. These are little charts with stick figures that show a social situation and give visual prompts of ways to handle it. You can find many examples by searching online using the term "social stories autism."

Leadership Gone Wrong

Kids, as they socialize, will test out social power. They form clubs, in-groups and out-groups. Benign clubs are great, but sometimes clubs can go wrong.

In some ways, children use clubs to learn leadership. But leadership, gone wrong, can cause very serious problems.

In one incident, a group of first grade girls started a hate club, naming a particular boy. This started on the playground at lunch, a time when teachers usually were not around. One little girl started this hate club and went around asking others to join.

The teacher got wind of this and was frankly appalled. These were 6- and 7-year-old kids. She took the girls aside and sat down to talk with them.

When this teacher had something serious to say, she would sit down in order to be at the kids' level. That way they could see her eyes better, and she wasn't looming over them. She made the message clear and short: "We do not do hate clubs."

After that discussion with the girls, the teacher talked to the whole class, using age-appropriate terms: "How would you feel if there was a hate club about you?"

As part of the discussion, she let them know that under no circumstances would this continue. Her expectations were high. This was going to end.

The teacher also saw this was serious enough to call the girls' parents, who agreed that this would not continue.

The teacher's particular attention went to the little girl who started it. She watched the little girl's face as she sat down to talk. What the teacher first saw was simply, "Uh-oh. I got caught." As they talked more, the girl realized this actually wasn't a good thing to do.

This girl was one of the leaders of the class and able to sway other people. She was testing her abilities, so it was important that she got immediate feedback that this kind of leadership was completely unacceptable.

The kids who start these things are often leaders, so you want to get them turned around quickly. Consider ways you might channel their leadership abilities in a positive direction.

Later, you might talk with the child privately: "It looks like you're a leader. How do you suppose a leader acts? Would you want a leader to be kind?" And so on. You can also think about putting natural leaders in charge of something, like part of the school play, where their role is to help other children.

Little girls love to skip, so you might provide some skipping ropes and teach her skipping songs she can teach to her classmates. One teacher pointed out that she found there was less inappropriate behavior at recess or lunch if she provided a tub of skipping ropes, along with trucks that could be used in the sandpit. But the rule was if kids didn't share and cooperate, she would put the toys away for a day. They learned to cooperate.

This same teacher would let children take outside a little tote bag containing books at various reading levels. That way they could read to themselves or to younger children. This technique also acknowledges the importance of literacy in children's lives.

Leadership skills are a wonderful asset. You want to help your students develop them in a positive way, and you want to address this as early as possible. Misguided leadership skills can cause a great many problems in the years ahead.

Dealing with Distraction

Kids aren't the only ones dealing with distraction in the schoolroom. Teachers can be besieged by distraction too. One teacher–mentor pointed out that teachers who had a low tolerance for distraction tended to have more discipline problems.

Think about it: if a teacher doesn't deal well with distractions, she's going to be more stressed, more overtaxed, and more irritable. This is rapidly going to show up as behavior problems from the children around her.

An elementary teacher has continual distractions. There's always some small thing that administration wants or an interruption to the lesson or questions from the kids. Someone spills their juice or needs to go to the bathroom. It's one interruption after another.

Some people find distractions irritating; if so, the classroom is full of irritations. Think back to the escalation chart. This teacher could move up the chart ahead of her students.

Many of the suggestions in this chapter limit the number of sheer interruptions. In some ways that effort is as important as sensible rules and routines. But interruptions will never go away entirely.

If you're dealing with small children, you'll need to improve your tolerance for distraction. If you want your students to practice being calm, you will have to go first.

Summing It Up:
High Points of Chapter Five

At early ages, school is new and can make children anxious. Establish your classroom as a safe space, where discipline issues are the exception and kids are accustomed to learning. The goal is building self-regulation. This means kids who practice self-discipline and teamwork, rather than you disciplining from above.

Establish clear rules and a schedule to minimize unpredictability.

Order wards off discipline problems. Keep an organized, predictable classroom.

This is the optimal time to establish safe, calm habits. Head off negative behaviors before they take root.

Have kids create the rules for their class. Examples may include "Be kind," "Complete your work," and so on. This improves buy-in and makes classmates more willing to remind one another of the rules.

Use teamwork and peer pressure. Kids need to belong. It's much better to have them remind each other how to behave than for you to continually do it.

Not everyone will cooperate. That's to be expected. The goal is to have the great majority of students working together so that only a limited number are acting out.

Reward positive behavior. A favorite activity with a parent is a better reward than a toy or some other object.

Adult attention is a form of reward. If you make a public display over negative behavior, you are asking for trouble. Keep negative attention private, but share positive attention publicly so kids know it's available.

Send a welcome letter to parents. Ask about their child's interests and concerns. This will provide you with a bridge to reach the child.

Keep parents in the loop by establishing two-way communication. Make sure parents know you're listening. If they know you want the best for their child, they are far more likely to cooperate if things are tough.

Techniques to build self-regulation include The Office (a separate quiet space) and a listening station (a place to record a complaint along with a chosen solution).

Tantrums may end sooner if you use few words, provide the child separate space (i.e., remove the audience), and remain calm.

Leaders will always be with you. They will be a force for good or bad, so guide them early. By definition kids are immature, so of course they make immature leaders. Show them the kind of leaders you want them to be.

Build up your tolerance for distraction. Distraction is a constant in the lower grades. Teachers who don't deal well with distraction tend to escalate.

CHAPTER SIX

Grades 3-6: Insights and Intervention

Hopefully by third through sixth grade, students have acquired basic skills for self-regulation and staying calm in school, but that doesn't always happen. The kid may have transferred in from another program or earlier teachers may have let things slide. Meanwhile, the kids are getting physically larger. They're no longer small kids throwing tantrums. They are increasingly capable of doing damage.

And sometimes kids scare adults. Remember, the escalation chart has two sides, and when adults get upset, escalation jumps.

In this chapter, we'll examine two stories of older children. The first one amounts to a master class on how to teach self-regulation in order to manage an unmanageable child. The second story, for more of a challenge, looks for guidelines in the middle of chaos.

Self-Regulation

Sometimes the problems in this age range exist because no one intervened earlier. We'll call this boy Jimmy. He'd been in the same school since kindergarten, throwing massive tantrums. The tantrums were so frequent and severe that teachers gave up and sent him home, over and over again.

Jimmy got older without learning to control his temper or even cope with school. After years of this, it fell to the third grade teacher to finally tackle the problem.

Jimmy's family was wealthy and quite privileged. When he first entered school his parents instructed the teachers: "Don't ever say no to him, because he doesn't like it. We don't ever do it."

When something was not to Jimmy's liking, he would throw a screaming tantrum, overturning desks and ripping things off the wall. And this child had to control everything: who sat near him, where he lined up, what he studied, everything. He was no better at home. His parents had a mini-van, and when he once didn't get the seat he wanted, he kicked in the panels.

Jimmy was too much for most teachers. They couldn't contain him and teach the class, so they usually sent him home. This might happen several times a week.

Well, Jimmy wanted to be home: There were no rules, he could have whatever he wanted, and he could play video games as much as he liked. It was becoming evident he had difficulty dealing with people. He had no friends. The gaming was starting to look like addiction, a compulsive way to moderate his moods.

By third grade, Jimmy was getting large enough to do real damage and had never learned the rudiments of self-regulation. No one expected it of him. At that point he entered Marta's class.

Marta had been hearing about this kid for years and suspected there might be nothing inherently wrong with Jimmy, except for his ability to manipulate adults. Jimmy had no friends, yet Marta found him quite likable when he wasn't losing control.

Marta decided this had to stop. This kid would have no future if he went on this way, and she wanted to see if he could be saved. She started by getting to know him.

Marta sometimes kept Jimmy in for recess, but in a friendly kind of way: "Jimmy, I want to talk with you a minute, stay and eat your apple." "Hang out with me at recess." At lunch, she'd pull up a chair and sit down with him.

Jimmy went along with this because he liked the attention. It was evident that his parents loved him, but it was unclear whether they liked him. There was another special-needs child at home, and Jimmy didn't get much positive attention.

Marta noticed that when Jimmy was out of control, he'd hit adults, but not other children. She suspected he actually wanted to have friends, but his behavior made it impossible.

When Jimmy totally went out of control, Marta couldn't intervene, because she'd get kicked or hit. Instead, she worked out a plan with the principal. There was no aide, so Marta would gather up the other kids and leave while the principal sat with Jimmy. She took away the audience. They had regular plans for the library, to read outside, or head to the gym. Jimmy got left behind. Jimmy wanted to be with other kids, so this began to have an effect.

As the tantrums began to scale down, Marta would say, "Jim, you lost control. Are you feeling calm enough now to join the group?" Since he really wanted to be included, this began to get through. At home, his parents would just close the door while Jimmy trashed his room. So Marta's positive attention was a big change for Jimmy, and it was working.

After a tantrum had subsided, Marta worked with him on self-regulation. She taught him to do deep breathing when he got wound up: breathing in through his nose, out through his mouth.

She also did the tantrum technique—sitting quietly alongside the child, putting her hand on his back, and encouraging him to breathe slowly. Of course, some schools don't allow physical contact, but Marta's did. The physical contact and stillness helped bring him down.

She also found that humor worked with Jimmy. Of all things, she discovered the boy had a great sense of humor. Outrageous behavior tends to overshadow the rest of the personality, so you never know who the kid is until he calms down enough to let his character show.

As Jimmy began to change his behavior, Marta and he would half-joke in class. She would playfully look at him with suspicion, and Jimmy would fold his hands and declare, "Mercy, Miss M., I'm innocent!" The kid turned out to be a charmer.

Meaningful praise also worked. Marta would never offer empty praise (Jimmy was getting that at home), but as Jimmy calmed down, Marta found more than just the sense of humor. Jimmy was good at writing. He had a way with words. Marta would say, "That's an interesting way to describe that."

None of this came easy. September and October were wild, but by November, Jimmy was coming around.

Parents

When a behavior problem is this severe, you want the parents on board, acting as a team. This isn't always easy.

Jimmy's parents had a reputation at school. They'd been verbally abusive and dismissive toward previous teachers. Most of the staff avoided them.

Jimmy's parents were used to being intimidating. Marta's usual approaches didn't work. For instance, she tried to appeal to their sense of fair play: "He's not just disrupting his own schooling, he's disrupting the other children."

The parents were blunt: They didn't care. It didn't matter to them what happened to the other students.

When one thing didn't work, Marta would try something else. Her belief was to always approach parents from a place of love: "I know you want a good life for Jimmy. He's going to need to control his temper if he's ever to get on in life or hold down a job."

The dad said, "He doesn't have to get along with other people. We have enough money that he doesn't need a job. If he really wants to work, I can buy him a software company."

Marta switched again, "But what if Jim is a parent? You'd want him to be the best kind of husband and father he could be. If he's going to have a good life, he has to be able to get along with people."

Well, this had no effect either. It became clear that the parents did not have friends of their own and were deeply unhappy people. They didn't seem to be able to picture a better life for Jimmy. Clearly, much of the problem with Jim was that his parents didn't know how to show warmth and affection.

Given their limits, Marta approached this as a learning experience for the parents as well. She kept things short; meetings ran no longer than 15 minutes. She'd let them vent, then discuss making just one change at home in the coming week.

She'd cover small chunks at a time. She'd give them one thought, like limiting his gaming time or talking with Jim over dinner. They lacked a physical connection with Jimmy, so she suggested simple things, like playing catch. She'd give them a week to process each small change before bringing up something else. They did not deal with stress well themselves, so she gave them a good block of time to process, talk among themselves, and try out the new behavior.

Marta was especially careful in her choice of words. When parents have as many limitations as Jimmy's, ill-advised comments can do a lot of damage. In situations like this, it can be too easy to say something critical and for parents to take only that one thing away, often repeating it to the kid. Jimmy had enough problems. So Marta planned in advance the words she would say at the next meeting.

As Marta talked with the parents, she would comment on Jimmy's good points. They didn't know he had a sense of humor or that he enjoyed jokes. She suggested they sit down at the computer with him and look up jokes on the Internet.

One thing made a clear impact on the parents: Jimmy started to get invited to birthday parties. This was new. Up to now, his behavior had been so out of control he never got invited anywhere. This was huge. The mother in particular appreciated it.

Through the rest of the year, Jimmy stabilized in class. The other kids came to enjoy his company. In many ways, he made more headway than his parents did.

At the end of the year Marta got a very nice gift and a card from Jim that said, "Thank you for liking me." She thought it very likely that she was the first adult who genuinely did.

Follow-up

Jimmy's story may have been a master class in how to help a child learn self-regulation, but the story doesn't have a perfect ending. The next year Jimmy came back to a new teacher and his friends. He managed this transition and did fine. His reputation had now changed at school, and other teachers could build on what Marta had done.

His parents, however, did not lock in the gains, and they made a terrible mistake. They assumed that now Jimmy was doing well, they could take his behavior for granted. For unrelated reasons they moved him to a different school, taking him away from his world and his friends.

Friends, connections, and predictability were key to Jimmy's stabilization. By taking that away, they took the foundation out from under him before he had the maturity to maintain the stability himself.

These parents had all the choices in the world. They simply didn't see that Jimmy needed to stay in a school where he was learning to be successful by controlling his temper and learning to compromise.

For better or worse, parents are the key to long-term gain. This isn't fair. Kids will pay the price for what the parents fail to see. But this is the reality we have to deal with.

The Relay Race

Teachers typically work alone in their classrooms, but not strictly in isolation. We help the child grow and learn, and then we hand him off to the next teacher. It's not a solo run—it's a relay race. The ultimate success can depend on how we pass the baton.

The baton has to go to a few different hands, including some who tend to drop it. This drives teachers frantic, which is understandable. You do all this work, you do everything right, and then someone else drops the baton. Teachers get distressed feeling that their hard work gets thrown away.

But it speaks to a basic truth: We do not get to choose the team. We can cultivate a team or enhance a team, but the players get handed to us. And some of the players are not as strong as we would want.

Teachers have an advantage over relay runners: We can bring in back-up. Look around and see if there are ways to add to the team. Are there other family members, anyone stable who can be recruited? New team members can't be added to a relay race, but as educators, we often have the option of adding backup.

Fatal Flaw/Unique Gifts

Jimmy's parents were not easy to like. Oddly, their child turned out to be very likable. The parents seemed to have given up on being liked, even by each other. Their child wanted very much to be liked. At the young age of eight years, he was succeeding at what his parents couldn't do. This was so unlike the parents, they didn't know what to make of it. Ultimately, they couldn't support that gift.

The parents did not know how to like their kid. And they didn't set limits or offer the positive reinforcement and encouragement that would allow Jim to fit in socially at school. Marta found the key to the puzzle: Jimmy wished to be liked.

Think in terms of supply and demand. Positive attention and being liked was in painfully short supply, and so this kid ended up doing a great deal to get it.

Empty flattery was available every day, so it was worthless. Being liked was in short supply and so had high value. Work with whatever has high value to the child.

The Element of Surprise

By this age, most kids know too much about what's wrong with them. Troubled kids may not hear about much else.

Surprise the kid: tell them what's right. You may have to lie in wait for the moment that kid allows a talent, an interest, or a flash of positive behavior to shine through.

Kids themselves may know they have some particular strength or gift. But if a kid is seriously troubled, he or she may have no idea that it matters. For instance, a girl may know she's smart, and simultaneously believe it makes absolutely no difference in life or in what happens to her.

Pointing out when she does something well may surprise her and win you that momentarily puzzled look. That's opportunity, what one psychologist refers to as a "window in."

A troubled kid may be so unaccustomed to approval she has no idea what to make of it. That's OK, too. It's enough that you said something puzzling. Sometimes, as if you were luring wild birds, it's best not to chase. Let the "birds" get curious about you.

Do not lie. False flattery is insulting. And besides, these kids are used to being lied to. There's no surprise in empty compliments. Wait if you have to; then offer a positive comment when you have something valid to say.

Doing and Seeing

Now we'll turn our attention to the second story, which is also about a boy out of control. This case didn't go as well, but it too offered unexpected opportunity.

Jimmy's case was more about what to *do*—and how all adults need to follow up. Marta had insights into this boy, apart from all the uproar, and she used her insight to construct an action plan.

This next case is more about what to *see*. Until the adults can see beyond the uproar, they can't be effective or plan next steps.

Uproar is blinding. Violent outbursts grab our attention and trick us into overlooking crucial signals. We have to train ourselves to notice more than just the uproar—despite the noise.

For instance, in the last case, Marta noticed that Jimmy would lash out and destroy things, but he would not strike out at other kids. He craved friends; he was lonely. This insight was essential to reaching him.

It's easy to pay attention when the fight starts; be sure to also pay attention to when the fight stops. If a fight turns on and off, you've been presented with meaningful clues.

Max's Story

This is the case of an 11-year-old boy we'll call Max. He had been taken out of school for punching teachers and aides, kicking things, and running out of the classroom. Like Jimmy, he lashed out at adults, not kids.

Max lived alone with his mother who tried to home-school him, but he only got worse. Eventually he had to be hospitalized. After a stint in treatment, Max was judged to be stable enough to be mainstreamed with counseling support. This was to be his first step back, via a meeting with his new counselor. We'll call the counselor Ann.

As this plays out, keep track of how the fight starts and stops.

As the elevator opened on Max and his mom, both of them were yelling. Max didn't want a new therapist. He liked the old one. Mom was yelling for him to shut up, that he'd ruin things. Max was already kicking and punching his mom, who was not a big woman. Max was a big kid.

Ann, the counselor, needed to calm things down, so she offered to have Max hang out in the hallway. There were toys in the hall, and Ann had things to discuss with his mom. There was no need to rush things. Ann took Mom inside the counseling room, and left the door open to keep an eye on Max.

Mom was agitated, embarrassed, and angry, but Ann talked her down. Ann was not worried; after all, this was just the first step. Outside, Max calmed down. Pretty soon, he edged around the doorway, curious about a large, elaborate dollhouse in the room. He asked if he could play with the dollhouse.

Ann gave him permission, but his mom started to criticize the way he was playing. The two quickly ramped up, and as Ann put it, "The world vanished."

The mom started yelling at Max that he was going to blow it again, and Max started to punch himself. Mom tried to restrain him, but he broke away, now kicking the wall. He looked both upset and ashamed.

Ann, trying to calm things down, said, "He's not hurting anyone. This is the start of our work, it's OK. Maybe it's time to call it a day." No one heard this at all. Mom grabbed Max in a bear hug, but the boy broke away and shoved her backwards. Mom landed hard, on the sofa.

This was not a large room. By the time it got this physical, Ann called for backup, but no one answered. Now she started to get alarmed.

Mom and kid started pounding on each other. Mom kept trying to wrap the kid in a bear hug, while Ann tried to intervene. Then mom got her hands around the kid's neck in a stranglehold. In a moment or two the kid utterly collapsed, falling to the ground, wailing.

Half the building was outside the door. This was a thundering brawl, and someone called 911.

The counselor's supervisor took Max's mom down the hall to talk her down, and once she left the room the boy settled down. When his mom came back, he escalated. So far as Ann could tell, the sight of his mom set him off more than anything his mother actually said. When she went out of sight around the doorway, he'd quiet down again, even though he could still hear her in the hall.

Soon the paramedics arrived. The boy saw the stretcher and lit up, saying, "I'm going back to the hospital?" And he happily climbed on the gurney and let them strap him in.

The counselor, meanwhile, was in shock. Max's mom filed a police report with a cop, and while she was busy, Ann called the child services hot line. She really felt this ought to be investigated.

When Ann went downstairs, Mom was waiting in the reception area. Ann said, "You know, we'll need to talk tomorrow about what happened."

The mother replied, "You know when I strangled him I wasn't doing it hard. It was just like this." And mom wrapped her hands around Ann's neck and pressed hard on her larynx. It really hurt.

Mom smiled, "See—it wasn't hard," then she turned and left.

Max's Story in Retrospect

This was one of those cases where you really had to wonder who most needed help, the kid or the parent.

Let's look at Max's behavior first. He's the crucial one in the room, the one whose future is at stake. That kid turned on and off like a switch.

When Max was out of sight of his mother, he calmed down. They didn't even need to close the door. These two had a powerful, learned reaction that was primarily visual. What was said wasn't nearly as important as the combination of sight and criticism. They went from zero to sixty with extraordinary speed.

You also could see the family history playing out. The bear hug worked when Max was small, but now he was a lot bigger. He needed space, and he wasn't getting it. When he did get space, he calmed down. Even when he went to the hospital he calmed down. When his mom tried to physically control him, he escalated through the roof.

Case Comparison

Comparing the cases of Jimmy and Max, a few points jump out.

Both kids can de-escalate. In Jimmy's case, the teacher was keenly aware anytime he made progress calming down, and she reinforced that progress. Max's mom was lost in her own flooding. She didn't notice when Max made progress and didn't know how to build on it.

Once flooding comes into play, noticing is harder than you'd think. Remember the advice of the wise nun-mentor: Use your eyes to observe. You can't change what you can't see.

Max's mom is working a lot harder than Marta and not getting nearly the results. It's not for lack of love; Max's mom is even willing to risk her physical safety. Marta is getting better results because she asks, observes, and guides her strategy based on Jimmy's responses and desires. Max's mom seems to automatically oppose what her son wants.

Some of the things kids want are bad for them. Other things are noisy, but harmless. Pick your battles.

Marta thought through her strategies. She watched carefully to see what worked with Jimmy and followed up with positive reinforcement. Max's mom was flooding too much to think at all. She was running on sheer reflex, and it wasn't working. The successful batter stays ahead of the pitch.

Max's mother did not notice when things got better. She must have paid good money to get that kid into a hospital, yet she didn't seem to notice that his behavior had changed. In fact, most of Max's promising behaviors were overlooked entirely.

Parenting Skills

Max's mom had a set of strategies to de-escalate the fight, and they weren't working. In fact, they were frankly disturbing. Her attempts to gain control drove things out of control.

Criticism. Criticism is one of the least promising ways to de-escalate anything. With Max, it was like dropping a match in gasoline. Mom repeatedly stated her anxiety: don't ruin this. She *so* did not get what she wanted.

Think with your hands. The bear hugs may have worked in some fashion when Max was smaller. But once he got bigger, the technique didn't work at all. In fact, it obviously made him panic. Control became a paradox: The harder she forced control, the wilder the kid became.

Meanwhile, look at *when* the mom exerted control: It was not at the point of any harm. She exerted control when she felt embarrassed. For instance, she grabbed Max when he kicked the wall; yet the counselor clearly stated it didn't matter. It was the counselor's wall, and the wall was designed to be kicked. But once the mom became distressed she radically escalated.

This mom could not contain her own flooding, and her default solution was to act with her hands. Modeling is the most powerful form of teaching. This kid is being taught that overpowering others is the way to solve problems. As he grows bigger, that lesson will lead to disaster.

Brute force. This happens when parents are beyond their limits. When Mom choked the kid, he collapsed and wailed. All the fight went out of him, instantly.

Chokes don't work that fast. That was also learned behavior. This clearly was not the first time Mom had choked him into submission. Ann was absolutely right to call child services.

Mom's Plan A was criticism, and her Plan B was a bear hug. When both of those failed, Plan C was choking. Mom may have been desperate, but this was a disaster in motion.

Managing perceptions. This is a sophisticated adult strategy. Mom knew she'd gone too far, so she went back and justified: "You know when I strangled him I wasn't doing it hard." And then, since she thought with her hands, she proceeded to choke the counselor.

The counselor was too dumbstruck to respond. This would be time for a reality check: "Yes, that did hurt. I'm filing a police report."

Adults and Police

When possible, we try to steer kids away from the police. But adults live under different rules. When an adult lays violent hands on you, you get to call the police, and it's probably the right thing to do.

You deserve a safe workplace, but it's also for the good of the kid. If this kind of behavior is coming toward you, there is almost certainly violence happening at home. Ann was already witness to some of this.

Something needs to get through to this parent. Adults can't be put in detention. You have to make the point that physical violence is not accepted, in any way, under any conditions. The out-of-control parents have to stop acting this way, for the good of everyone.

Someone accustomed to violence may find this a difficult concept. They've become accustomed to a totally different set of standards. Bringing in the police is a wake-up call. Whatever else happens, the report will go on record, so that if the kid needs to bring charges later, there will confirming documentation.

Kid Strategies

Max also used a number of strategies, and they were considerably better than his mom's strategies. He was using child skills, so they weren't sophisticated strategies, but they're still worth noting.

Yelling. This scenario opened as Max objected loudly to leaving his former therapist. The counselor may have missed a move here. We look for bonds and the willingness to attach in order to bring down behavior. He'd made friends with the prior counselor, and now he was losing that bond. Could there have been some way to manage the change without it feeling like a loss? The baton was being passed, which is often a difficult moment, and much of the fight was about control: perhaps Max should have been consulted about the change.

Space. When Max had space, he calmed down. Once the counselor took Mom aside and left Max alone to play, he played nicely. After a while he grew curious about the huge dollhouse and ventured into the room. He asked if he could play with things. This kid had manners. When given space to make voluntary choices, his behavior markedly improved.

Hitting things, not people. As the mom escalated and tried to control Max, he hit himself, then turned and started kicking the wall. Kicking a wall is common, a way of relieving flooding; the wall was built to be kicked. The counselor was ahead of it all, and there was no harm in it.

It didn't become harmful until the moment Max's mom tried the bear hug.

Thrashing. Once Mom used the bear hug, the 11-year-old threw her off. He yelled at her to keep away, but that didn't work. This child was learning that brute force was the only way to get space. This is dangerous.

This kid rapidly de-escalated again once he had space, with his mom in the hallway. The lesson that needed to be reinforced is that he could be successful by using words, not his hands. You need an 11-year-old to learn that words work, that words matter, and that words can deliver safety.

Collapse. When all else utterly fails, a human may give up. This kid collapsed in a puddle and wailed. At least the fight was over.

Unfortunately, both sides showed learned behavior. The mom had learned that choking works. The child had learned that brute force was the final answer.

Cooperation. When the paramedics arrived, this kid happily went with them. The rage was forgotten.

Whatever they were doing at the hospital, they were doing something right. As a rough guess, this probably included standard processes like listening to the boy, positive reinforcement, giving him space, and not touching him if he was blowing off steam without hurting anything.

While it's startling how fast this kid escalated and de-escalated, it's unclear if this is particularly "crazy." If Mom criticized him, Max jumped to anger. If Mom laid hands on him, Max went berserk. Once he got space, Max behaved like a startlingly normal child. If there was anything truly unusual about the kid, it's the speed at which he switched gears.

Desperate children will do desperate things. They don't have the skills yet to come up with a better plan. Even so, compared with the parent, this kid had better skills, possibly skills learned at that hospital. Like Jimmy in the last story, he was absorbing new lessons faster than his parent.

Curiosity

After Max was left alone in the hallway, he became curious about the room with everyone else. He was intrigued by the dollhouse and asked if he could check it out.

This was a giant clue: curious kids aren't escalating. Curiosity is a sign they have reached calm, although it doesn't guarantee that they're stable.

Think of the verbal flags in escalation: Hostility is all about "you" with a laser focus. Anger is about "you" in the general sense. Anxiety is about "me." Only at calm does someone get outside themselves to see what the rest of the world has to offer.

Max wasn't curious as they arrived at the new office; he was focused on fighting with his mom. He also wasn't curious about meeting the new therapist; he was still focused on arguing. Left alone, he started playing quietly and then poked his head around the corner to see about everything else. He was curious, and he wasn't fighting anyone.

Teachers intuitively use curiosity any number of ways. When a small child is lost in a tantrum, you can put a brightly colored favorite toy nearby, to draw her out of herself. When the child focuses on something outside herself, the tantrum subsides.

Older kids with behavior issues can be captivated by computers. Technology is an endless source of curiosity. And no, they won't learn well-rounded people skills from a computer, but building on their curiosity about computers isn't a bad first step when you're teaching them not to explode.

Nevertheless, all technology is not created equal. For instance, aggressively addictive computer games do not improve calm. They usually involve just blasting one thing after another. And mindlessly repetitively computer games, like solitaire, don't spark curiosity. They just have a numbing effect. To use technology to move toward de-escalation, look for something that sparks curiosity and gets the kid out of his own head.

Yes, there will be a time the kid has to deal with his own feelings, but the midst of a raging fit is not that time. First get the kid calm, then stable. Finally, talk things through in order to lock-in stable skills.

Fear

The adult side of the escalation chart has a great deal of meaning for teachers who work with kids who've been labeled as aggressive, defiant, developmentally disabled, or autistic. It is too easy to fear these kids, and once fear takes hold of us, we start missing signals. That means we lose our chances to take advantage of opportunities to de-escalate, or that we inadvertently escalate the situation ourselves.

The same can be true in our dealings with parents. Once we've had an unfortunate episode with a parent, it's too easy to let that troubling memory drive our emotions and color our future interactions. We stop noticing what they do well and only see what they do wrong.

The same effect holds true for parents as they deal with us. After bad news or a bad experience with us, they may feel aggrieved, indignant, and misunderstood. Trouble begins when these feelings blind them to the real possibilities in moving forward with us to do the best for their kid.

Too often, fear controls what we see. And frankly, fear doesn't see much. Fear misses cues left and right.

You'll notice that the teachers who are most effective at handling troubled kids are those who aren't afraid. It doesn't seem to matter if this lack of fear comes from inner confidence or ironclad faith; the ones who are most effective are those who aren't scared.

Cultivate the ability to notice not only what kids do wrong but also what they do right, even when fear or uproars attempt to distract you. You'll be rewarded by finding new solutions for yourself and for your students.

Summing It Up:
High Points of Chapter Six

Conflict is stressful and upsetting, which undermines clear observation. Your success with intervention depends on your ability to see past distractions.

It's all right if you notice important clues only in retrospect; disruptive behavior tends to repeat. You may do better the second time around.

Cues from Kids

Watch for what the child does and what the child *doesn't* do. Targets of aggression, circumstances, and triggers that touch off conflict can all provide important clues.

Know what the child values before you attempt to alter behavior. You can get more done, with less opposition, if you're guided by what the kid wants.

Watch when a fight stops, as well as when it starts. When a fight switches on and off, you are presented with valuable information.

Be alert for setbacks if the child's world is disrupted. Make sure support is available to get behavior back on track.

Negative skills for kids include chaotic yelling, thrashing, lashing out, capitulation or collapse. These are skills that reflect desperation, but they may result in disaster as the child gets older.

Even negative skills are an attempt to fulfill some need. They can be important clues because the more you understand those needs, the better you can reach the child.

Watch for any positive skills a child does have. They may give you clues to a child's hopes and values. Make the most of a child's positive skills that exist here and now.

Curiosity is a sign the child is not escalating. This is an important marker. Work with it.

Teacher Responses

It's crucial to show kids that alternate skills work. Kids have to experience the results of better skills before you can expect them to replace old, destructive skills.

Allow time to lock in changes. Improvements in behavior may reach a plateau, but that's different from permanent stability. Don't be lulled into taking improvements for granted.

Fear controls what you see. As you look back on a situation, you have the opportunity to calm down and see things you missed in the crisis of the moment. Deliberately induce calm to improve your insight.

Fear wrecks judgment. Adults may fear chaos, losing face, even noise. These are additional reasons our judgment may improve in retrospect.

Working with Parents

Negative skills for adults include dismissing the child, reflexive criticism, physical restraints, brute force, or managing perception rather than improving behavior. These skills hardly inspire sympathy, but may mask desperation in the adult.

Work in small blocks of time. Present one small action step at a time. Let parents have at least a week before the next action step.

Choose your words ahead of time. An ill-advised word can be turned into a weapon and used against the child.

Parents may have difficulty supporting a child's goals that are different from their own. Explain and translate the child's goals.

You may need to explain a child's positive points to an exhausted parent.

Working with kids isn't a solo race, but a relay. You'll have to pass the baton. This is a moment that can introduce an error. Be careful.

Consider others who might help support the child if parents simply cannot manage.

CHAPTER SEVEN

Middle School: Fighting

At this point, we can build on all our previous work with flooding, behavior patterns, and intervention, and bring it to bear in order to get kids to stop fighting.

By middle school, most kids are big enough that someone could get seriously hurt. Moreover, consequences are changing. At 13 or 14, a scuffle can still be handled at the school level. By 16 or 17, a fight can bring the police.

By middle school it becomes crucial to get these kids on a different track. You need to get them to stop fighting and to start making better choices.

Step Back

Of course if two kids are slugging it out, you'll be tempted to jump in the middle. You're the teacher, so you feel you should be in control. But consider a moment before you so do. If your students outweigh you by 50 pounds, this isn't safe. If you get injured, it doesn't help your students, and it can considerably complicate matters.

One young teacher, enthusiastic but small, had two big eighth-graders break into a fight. She jumped in, and one pushed her away, half-trying to protect her. But pumped with adrenaline, he knocked her across the room. She hit the wall and hurt her back. She had to go to the hospital, which meant the police were called in. What would have been a simple fight resulting in detention turned into expulsion and an arrest record.

Of course every teacher wishes to be in charge; it's what teachers do. But physically throwing yourself in the middle of a fight isn't a good plan. Every school district has a protocol for handling fights, and it's important that you follow it. You don't help anyone by getting hurt yourself.

Stopping a Fight Before It Starts

The best time to break up a fight is before it happens. Even with Max, the 11-year-old in the last chapter whose conflict with his mother resulted in the police being called, the counselor saw the moment when the kid and his mom went to total focus. Some people describe this phenomenon as, "The world dropped away." This is the red flag. A fight is imminent.

According to Max's counselor, at least 60 seconds passed from that moment of total focus until the situation spun out of control. That can be a long time in a fight. It's like the suspended animation people experience in a car wreck. You know what's going to happen, but it hasn't happened yet. This is your window of opportunity.

So, the would-be fighters are intensely flooding and locked on each other. Break the visual lock; break their eye contact. Flooding people are easily distracted, so throw a distraction. This is not unlike a torero in a bullfight (also, in fact, a rodeo clown, but let's go with the image of torero).

The students are flooding so they won't easily hear you. Yell their names. Stay out of reach, at least two arm-lengths away. Motion your hands apart and shout simple directions: "Back up! Back up! Back up!" As you yell this, move sideways. Model what you want them to do: physically move and wave them away from each other. The goal is to reach the mirror neurons.

The sign that this is working is that the students will look at you, half-confused, unsure whether to obey you or fight. This is also like the action in a bull ring—the moment when the bull is unsure which choice to make. This is good; you're halfway there. Hold their attention, keep working them: "Back up! Back up! Back up!"

A point in your favor is that the would-be combatants are often less invested in the fight than they appear. This may be particularly true in bad neighborhoods. It's important not to lose face, but in bad neighborhoods, fights are scary. Students might not mind if a teacher gives them an excuse to back out. Yet they have to save face while doing this. They may grudgingly back up, as if for your sake, but not because they're afraid.

If you can stop the fight before it gets physical, many important things happen:
1. Your would-be fighters have just learned that when an adult shouts, it's their cue to back up. Remember, flooding is learned behavior. You want to implant a safe reflex. If they've done it once, you can use this cue again. A reflex of stepping back at the point of rage could keep them out of jail someday—or out of the hospital.
2. They controlled themselves in a fight. They went awfully close, but ultimately, they didn't brawl. This is huge, so reinforce it before you give them detention.

3. You have shown the rest of the class how to stop a fight. They'll be talking about it for months.
4. You've just done terrific work picking up cues, choosing the right timing, and acting in the window of opportunity. There should be medals for this. There aren't, but you deserve one.
5. You've improved your "street cred." This will be useful if you ever need to do it again.

"Dissing" and the Honorable Out

In this technique, we'll still take advantage of the muddy thinking caused by flooding and use this confusion to interrupt the fight. But this time we'll tie in issues of respect and disrespect, since that's what drives many fights anyway.

You see two kids with the jutting jaws and intense focus of kids about to fight. Choose the one who least wants to fight, and bark your order at him: "Roman! Didn't I just tell you to go feed the tarantula? Right now! Go!"

This will break the locked eye contact, at least for Roman. Now Roman, perhaps not being the quickest kid in living memory, may object that, in fact, you never told him to feed the tarantula. Don't let that bother you: "I'm telling you now. Go!"

Roman now has an excellent excuse to walk away from the fight. With Roman safely out of the way, you call the more aggressive student over to you.

"Jackson, I would like to be mistaken. For a moment there, I thought you were about to punch Roman. You wouldn't dream of doing anything that disrespectful in my class, would you?"

You're throwing a complicated idea at Jackson during a time when his mind isn't working well. You're saying the situation is not about his anger at Roman. You're saying that fighting in class is disrespectful to you, and you're not having it. You're also saying that you are the alpha, this is your territory, and you will decide what behavior is acceptable.

Roman is now a side issue. This is between you and Jackson. But you've given Jackson an excellent way to back down: You could be mistaken. Jackson would not be that disrespectful. And it's easy for Jackson to agree because flooding people are highly suggestible.

You then reinforce the positive: "I'm glad to hear that Jackson. You've got a good head on your shoulders, and I'd like to see you make something of yourself."

Watch for Jackson blinking rapidly or his eyes slewing sideways as he processes your words. You may also see his head make a slightly jerky movement. This is all good; it means a new idea is getting through. Give him time to complete the process; don't interrupt.

From here, find positive ways to reinforce Jackson, to give him an honorable role in your territory. The negative is not enough: you've just agreed that he would not be so disrespectful as to fight in your class. But he now needs a positive: he is so honorable that his place is to, say, lend you a hand at recess. Or help someone else with math.

Even in the roughest neighborhoods, being disrespectful—"dissing" is a powerful social value. "Dissing" is everywhere. But a clear path to honor is hard to find. You provide that path, and make it a path suited for Jackson.

Just a word of reinforcement: In order to claim your rights as alpha and define your territory, you must look the part of the alpha. You need the straightforward posture, low voice, and the demeanor of benevolent but firm command. You cannot define the rules of your territory with a squeaky voice, while dancing side to side. Your look of command is needed to bring Jackson around.

The Talk

Once the fight is broken up—however your school board prefers—you'll have to give the kids involved the proverbial "talk." The typical purpose is to scold, find out who threw the first punch, or expel everyone involved. However, another worthwhile goal is to make this a learning experience for the kids, to prevent this kind of thing in the future.

Consider it also a learning experience for you. You want to get the most good out of it in order to help keep similar fights from happening in the future.

If the kids are still pumped with adrenaline, give them something physical to do. In some schools, it might be two laps around the school grounds. Earlier we talked about the assistant principal who had kids lift a stack of books. Whatever it is, start with some way to physically drop their adrenaline before you attempt to talk with these kids. You want their brains clear, and they won't be able to hear you with their minds spinning and wired.

Adrenaline and Truth

In the first chapter we discussed ways that adrenaline magnifies. This distortion can start fights. A kid may be telling the truth as she knows it but still have a skewed point of view. She may have heard insults that were not meant as insults or perceived a threat that really wasn't there. If the kid believes she's being "dissed," she can quickly jump to that conclusion.

Someone in the grip of adrenaline may also talk globally: "She's always on my case." "She never lets me walk past her in the hallway without taking a shot at me." Well, of course that's not accurate: "always" and "never" are hard to carry off. Nonetheless, under adrenaline, it may feel like always and never. Don't give this kid a hard time. She's telling the truth as she knows it, and if you give her a hard time about it, she may give up on talking with you at all.

It's all right to talk about a misunderstanding, to suggest that possibly a comment wasn't taken well or that something was said in the wrong tone of voice. That's valid, and once the adrenaline loosens its grip, the student might accept that fine distinction. Pointing out such fine distinctions can also leave both sides a way to apologize while saving face. And last but not least, the ability to gauge fine distinctions can keep someone out of a fight, so it's important that students start developing those skills.

Stepping Through the Fight

You may have a few kids who fight repeatedly. Being teachers, we often assign essays to these kids: we want them to think things through. And we're likely to get back essays that read, "I shouldn't have punched Charlie. I'm really sorry." But then in a month or two he punches Charlie again, or maybe he punches Al. So the "thinking through" process hasn't really happened.

The reality is that kids who fight may not be good with words. Asking them to talk it through or write about it may not be effective. One alternative is to have kids draw pictures with comments, like a scene from a comic book or graphic novel.

Another alternative is to have them step through the fight. This can work even if they're not great with words. Have them show you what happened, step by step, and say what they were thinking at each point.

This can teach you far more about what started the fight than just having them talk or write about it. They may have very little idea of what's driving them. Aggressive people tend not to know themselves very well and lack insight into their own behavior. This could be an opportunity for them to gain some awareness.

At this point you are *not* looking for holes in the story. You are looking for insights, points at which the fight could have been stopped.

So you place them: Howard is here. Charlie is there. Howard puts his chin out, and says something. Ask Howard: "OK, what's going through your mind?" Then it's Charlie's turn: "Where are you? You hear this. What do you do? What's in your mind?"

For these kids, talking about motivation is not exactly easy. Asking them to step through the fight and say one sentence at each stage is a more workable plan. Their bodies will remember more about the fight than they do.

By the way, do *not* do this until they are both stable and thoroughly calmed down. If they're still flooding, the fight may break out all over again.

After they're done stepping through the fight, you can discuss it: "OK guys: Where could you have done things differently? If something like this happens again, at what point could you head off the fight?"

Find something for both sides to do differently. You want some solid suggestions from both of them.

Then you can assign your essay: "I want you to write down what you've figured out in this room. What would you do differently if there were a next time?"At this point, you might get an interesting essay that helps kids solidify their new insights.

Clues

As you have the kids step through the fight, pay attention to clues. This can help you head off future fights.

For instance, when we stepped through fights in psychiatric units, we found that staffers were apt to be attacked at the doorway, going into a patient's room. It became clear that this was about territory; patients were defending their space.

Even though these were public hospitals, a patient's room was all the space he or she had. Staff assumed they could walk in and out at will, since it was their workplace. But that's not how the patients felt at all.

So we instituted a new rule: Knock before entering a patient's room. Ask to come in. If the answer isn't, "Yes," stay outside the doorway. We no longer had these fights.

Your school has different territories, whether or not students live there. You can look for clues anywhere: Did someone have room to back up? Did someone hear an insult that possibly wasn't there? If an insult was there, why? Look for triggers. Then, as the adult, talk them through different ways to disarm that trigger.

Once a kid says something wrong, he may not have the skills to back up. As an adult, you will have some better ideas.

Denials

In the course of stepping through the fight, Howard might say, "I didn't touch him." You can point out that Charlie is looking a little banged up for never having been touched. If Howard persists in denying everything and glares at Charlie as if to dare Charlie to contradict him, consider: Where do you suppose Howard learned this behavior? First guess is from a bully or from domestic violence at home. So it's actually very important to interrupt this: "Howard, look at me. We're not going to play it like that."

Suppose that you are talking with two students about their fight. Your goal is to have them behave like honorable adults, but you need to speak with them in a way that they understand. Appeal to their sense of growing up to be stand-up, or honorable, adults.

You might ask Howard, "Do you know what a mind game is? How would you describe a mind game?" Then ask Charlie. "Charlie, how would you describe a mind game?"

Explain: "We're not going to do mind games, because real adults don't do mind games, and I want you to grow up to be stand-up adults. You want to be a stand-up adult? OK, we start now."

If these kids have a history of problems, it's entirely likely no one has ever explained how stand-up individuals face responsibility. They may have no clear idea what it is to be an adult or how to start acting like one.

Apologies

Once you've sorted through the fight and discovered some things to do differently, it's time for another teaching moment: the apology.

If we're still with Howard and Charlie, you can say something like: "What do you suppose a stand-up adult would do to set things right? Apologize like an adult. Do you know what it looks like to apologize like an adult?"

This may be a foreign concept. They may have never seen adults give a sincere and forthright apology.

We can force kids to apologize. It means nothing. The words are reluctantly spoken, and the fight may re-ignite as soon as your back is turned. Many kids don't know what an honest apology looks like. It's not as if we often see them from public officials. In a world where many kids fight at the hint of being disrespected, the art of apologizing with dignity can be a foreign concept. So one of the best things you can do is to model a decent apology.

A counselor was working with a group of clients with drug issues, and there was an adult there, a man she didn't like much. Professionally, that shouldn't matter; they still needed to work together.

They locked horns one day, and she said some regrettable things. He provoked her, but that was not the point. She was the professional; he was the client.

She was about to really go off when she heard her tone of voice. She stopped. Her jaw dropped, her head turned to the side, and she realized what she was about to say. She came back in a different tone of voice, and apologized. She said she had no right to talk to him that way, that she had let her emotions get out of hand, and that she knew she was not supposed to behave that way. So she apologized.

She was about to go back and pick up the discussion where they left off, but the rest of the group stopped her. They wanted to know how she backed up. How did she do that? What was going through her mind? How did she know she was acting badly?

The counselor realized her clients had never before seen someone apologize with dignity. They acted like they'd seen a unicorn. Watching someone act out was an everyday occurrence. Watching someone brazen it out or lie was no big deal. But watching someone catch themselves, stop, change course, and apologize was a revelation.

The counselor turned it into a teaching moment, and they spent the rest of the session talking it through. She broke it into pieces for them. "I caught something about my behavior—my tone of voice—then I suddenly realized I had a pounding headache. I remembered my standards. I thought about the right thing to do. Then I had a plan, so I knew what to do."

Like those clients, kids who fight may have never seen this kind of decent, forthright apology. Apologizing with dignity, or backing off a bad position, is a skill that even many top leaders haven't managed. You can model how it's done. It's an important social skill to have.

Who's Telling the Truth?

Often, when you have two kids talking about a fight, each one says the other one started it. After they've stepped through it, perhaps the stories still don't match. You have to decide who's telling the truth—or the closest thing to it.

It may be tempting to just split the difference. Given the distortions of adrenaline, both students could be telling the truth as they see it; it's also true that they both could have started it. However, in order to make this a true learning opportunity, you need to make sense of this somehow.

Judges have to wrestle daily with this problem of sorting truth from fiction. I've had the pleasure of working with judges on this, and they have interesting things to say.

Many people feel they can accurately sense when someone's lying: "I can't really describe it, but you just know." They might be picking up on physical tics or gestures—in poker these are known as "tells." But as kids get older and gain practice lying, it can be much harder to be sure who's telling the truth.

Research has not yet been able to find any consistent gestures in lying. That's really not surprising. If a sign of honesty is to look you squarely in the eye, a skilled liar will do exactly that. You may remember from your own school days, skilled liars were beginning to emerge by fourth or fifth grade.

Most of the signals we associate with lying are also associated with fear or discomfort; in short, the submissive signals we covered earlier. These include averting the eyes, fidgeting, shifting uneasily, biting the lips, and so on. But there are many reasons a kid would feel scared and uncomfortable when standing before an authority. So these gestures don't necessarily point to lying.

Sometimes someone who is lying will briefly brush their own nose. It's physiology. When you're exposed to something you don't like or doing something you don't approve of—like lying—the capillaries in the nose change, and your nose will itch. Consequently you brush your nose. This can be a fleeting gesture, a fraction of a second.

You can test this yourself the next time you lie—say, making a lame excuse for not cleaning the garage. You may notice your nose itches.

The reason that brushing the nose isn't proof of a lie is that the same response can be triggered by anything that person doesn't approve of, such as tattling on one's best friend. So while it's certainly a sign of disapproval, there's no way to be sure it's a sign of lying.

Another sort of micro-reaction may occur at the shift from a low stress statement—say, telling name and age—to a high stress statement, like lying. Sometimes it's a shift in timing, a tension that's hard to define. One judge described it as a sudden spark, a concentrated stillness; sometimes almost an animal alertness. Another judge described it as a feeling, "The game is on."

So these are indicators that something is up. But it's still up to you to discern the truth.

Shading the Truth

Ask detailed questions, and see if the details shift.

Kids who have made up a story often add or remove details even as they speak. Rather than tell the truth, they're working a line they hope will appeal to you. They will be watching your face carefully, checking to see how the story is going over. If your facial expression shows disbelief, they'll quickly erase that point and replace it with something more appealing.

It's easy to fall for this. After all, a made-up story can be much more compelling than the truth, and this story is tailored to appeal to you. For instance, the student may appeal to school pride or go on a charm offensive.

One sign of the manufactured story is that there may be too much emotion, and not enough fact. For instance, you may ask for a fact, and instead get a burst of outrage: "How can you say such a thing?! Would I do that?"

Ask again. If you keep asking for a fact and are not getting an answer, it may be because the truth won't go over well.

Social workers call these omissions "memory drops." Your young fighter may be detailed and accurate on many points, saying where he was, what time it was, and so forth. Then he may suddenly get vague about the start of the fight. He "can't remember." Conveniently, it will be pivotal things he can't remember. They've been deleted from the picture.

Keep in mind your own vulnerabilities, because this will influence what lies work on you. Ask yourself this question: In the past, who has lied to you successfully? Someone has; we have all been lied to, and at some point, some lie has worked.

Perhaps it was someone who appealed to your sense of fair play. Or maybe it was someone who appealed to your desire to protect, be in charge, or defend the reputation of your school.

Think through which lies penetrated your defenses. That's where you'll need to be most careful.

Tell the Story

Research has shown one reliable way to catch a lie. It involves telling the story.

When people make up a lie by shading the truth, they do a mental run-through. The run-through goes from beginning to end, the natural way to tell a story.

To catch a lie, try asking for details out of order: "So, just before this fight broke out you walked out the door—I'm sorry, clarify this for me. What happened just before you walked out the door? "

Someone telling the truth can pick out part of the memory and describe what they were doing. They can play a mental film and pull up separate scenes. But with a made-up story, it's much harder to skip to individual scenes. The liar almost always has to mentally run through the story from the beginning in order to come back to the point you asked.

Each subsequent answer also has to match all the previous lies that were told. This can require more story editing. It's tiring, and it's hard to keep it all straight.

If you want to test for this, ask for details towards the middle or the end. See if the student can answer your question in a reasonable time or if he suddenly develops memory drops.

Judges look for inconsistency. They may tactfully give someone a final chance: "I've asked for this information several times. I'm concerned that you're not using this opportunity to put your facts forward." Wait, and see if the student finally gives you a clear and unambiguous answer.

Later you may have to explain to the parents just why this young man is in such trouble. Here's a neutral way of putting it: "I asked Joe several times for his story. This is what undermined his credibility...." You are tactfully giving the parents some pointers on how their son shades the truth.

Fear Fighting

Sometimes fights get completely out of hand. You wonder what gets into these kids, and you can be shocked by the amount of damage they can do. It may help to know whether the fight is driven by anger or fear.

One teenage girl—we'll call her Jiff—ran afoul of a girl-gang at her school. Girls may not physically fight at your school, but in some places they do. And when they do, things can get serious.

The leader of this pack of girls was angry over some perceived slight and vowed to teach Jiff a lesson. Jiff was not the fighting kind, and she was scared half to death.

Jiff dodged the girls for about a week, but they finally caught up with her one day after school. The leader was waiting with a bunch of her friends, and they quickly surrounded Jiff. The leader stepped forward as her friends egged her on. The leader shoved Jiff and launched the fight. The next thing Jiff really knew, she had the leader on the ground, pounding her head into the sidewalk, and the leader's friends were panicked and pulling her off. Jiff had opened a gash on the leader's forehead. There was blood everywhere. The leader ended up needing several stitches over one eye.

This was not the kind of neighborhood where things got reported to the police, so the leader's family took this in hand. A raft of cousins now scoured the neighborhood looking for Jiff. She hid. She managed to get through the end of term by bolting home every night, dodging house to house. Fortunately school was nearly over for the year. She went to a different school the next fall.

Jiff knew she had gone too far. Leaving a scar on the other girl's face was serious, and this was the scariest girl in the school. By pounding her head on the sidewalk, Jiff might have killed the other girl. Jiff had no recollection of how she got there, and until the others pulled her off, she wasn't even aware that the leader was no longer a threat.

This was a fear fight. Blind panic had taken over. Jiff had no idea what she was doing.

A fear fight is more dangerous, not less dangerous, than a conventional fight. The indicators of a fear fight are:

An unlikely culprit. One of these kids—quite possibly the one doing most of the damage—has no experience fighting, has never been known as a tough kid, and isn't very strong. Like Jiff, she is truly amazed at what has happened.

Multiple attempts to escape. Jiff dodged the leader and her formidable friends for about a week before they caught up with her. She would have gone on dodging had she not been cornered. She did not want this fight, and her reasons were not high-minded: she was convinced she hadn't a prayer.

No line of escape. The leader and her gang surrounded Jiff. There was no way out.

There's no question you'll need to punish this kid, if only in the interest of fairness. In fact, you'll need to punish both of them. But bear in mind there's little to be gained by making an example of someone for fear fighting. Driven by panic, Jiff lost control. You can't plan for panic. There is also little likelihood she'll do this again.

Circle Fights

Jiff's fight shows a common configuration: a lone kid surrounded by enemies. I call this a circle fight. While Jiff's story took place in a rough neighborhood, a similar pattern turns up in British boarding schools, and it assuredly happens in a suburb near you.

The circle fight has some interesting dynamics that can tell you a lot about how to intervene to stop them in the future.

The kid who's the target ends up in the center. Picture the circle like a clock, with the one in the center facing twelve o'clock. At twelve o'clock is the leader of the pack. The leader calls the target's name, sparks the confrontation, and will probably step inside the circle to fight.

At six o'clock is the henchman. This one faces the leader, and if the target in the center is slow to fight, the henchman may shove the kid from behind to goad him into fighting. The henchman stays out of sight and does the dirty work. Watch out for the henchman. This one is really trouble.

At three and nine o'clock you tend to see the kids who are least invested in the fight. They may not particularly want to be there at all. They may not be strong enough to say, "No," because they don't want to be left out. They're followers, not leaders. They may be ambivalent, and more to the point, they could go either way. Three and nine o'clock are the weakest parts of the circle.

One or eleven o'clock are the most interesting parts of the circle. These kids are standing next to the leader, the one who's driving the fight. In this position you may find a kid who is actually trying to stop the fight, but may not have the skill. They may mutter to the leader out of the corner of their mouth, "C'mon, Bill. You don't want to bother." Or, "Look, he said he's sorry." (To target) "You sorry, dumb face?" This kid is walking a tightrope. He's working with the skills of a kid and trying to look like a team player, but he's actually trying to head this off.

When I was a youngster, I got caught in circle fights repeatedly. In one, I was with a boy who was the kind of kid who got beat up in that neighborhood, and we got surrounded by a bunch from another school. They were underage, drinking, and spoiling for a fight.

We were encircled, and the leader was at twelve o'clock. Of course we faced him: he spoke to us and commanded attention. As we were fencing and trying to talk our way out of this, at eleven o'clock was a youngster who kept talking about how drunk he was.

I realized this boy didn't want us to get beaten up but had no idea how to stop things. So I started joking with him: "How drunk are you? Are you drunk as a skunk? Are you drunk as two skunks? Are you drunk as two skunks falling down the stairs and singing the 'Star Spangled Banner'?"

Well, kids new to drinking find drunk jokes very funny. He started playing back, reeling to one side and walking in circles. Between us we got the whole group laughing, and they forgot about beating us up and wanted us to join the party. Youngsters can go from wanting to kill you to being your best friend in twelve seconds flat.

That kid at eleven o'clock saved our hides. He may not have had words to articulate that, but something bad was coming that he did not want to see happen. He didn't know how to intervene. He wasn't the leader and he didn't have great skills. But in his clumsy teen way, he was trying.

Roles

If, as a teacher or administrator, you deal with a circle fight, pay close attention to each student's position in the circle and exactly what role each student plays. The leader, as we've seen in other places, will probably go on being a leader. You had better find ways to re-direct that leadership, because this kid will probably be a force, for good or not.

If someone plays the role of the henchman, you definitely want to keep an eye on that kid. This is a mean and trouble-making role; the henchman does the dirty work while staying just out of sight. Perhaps this was an isolated incident, but be aware of this kid in the future. The henchman, with the leader, should be singled out for the worst punishment.

Look to the kids at three and nine o'clock. Did they do anything? Were they complicit in any other way, say, filming the attack for YouTube? They may be simple followers, but followers with bad judgment. What can you do to improve that judgment, or put them in with better leaders? If they had a complicit role, like filming the abuse, they absolutely should be punished in line with the worst offenders. This goes beyond simple bad judgment to callous encouragement.

Finally, check on the kids at eleven and one o'clock. Were they saying or doing things to mitigate the fight? Were they trying to prevent the fight, or were they shoulder-to-shoulder with the leader? If they were intervening for good, how can you build their skills? Are they the conscience of the group? They'll need to bear consequences as well, but these kids can be forces for good. How can you develop their skills?

Let me be clear: these dynamics do not excuse anything. Everybody in the circle needs to experience consequences. But consider what you wish to gain from the punishment and how you wish to guide these students for the future. You have a teaching moment. You should use it.

Sightlines

When I was a youngster and had to deal with trouble regularly, I would often use sightlines to disrupt attacks. For instance, I'd get surrounded by a gang. Well, gangs aren't of a single mind; they have to continually check in with one another to decide what to do. They can't say, "Joe, what do you think? Time to make our move?" Instead, they would glance to each other to coordinate.

I would disrupt their sightlines, so they couldn't check in. A gang—operating as a unit—has a disadvantage. Individual members may be bright, but the collective thinking is a little slow. By interrupting sightlines and coordination, I made the attacks difficult. They weren't prepared to think, re-think, and re-think again. I think they got tired. It was easier to let me make my exit.

By the way, if you work in a rough school, some of your kids who aren't in gangs may be quite wily at handling situations. You might talk to them sometime about how they do it. Everyone has a system, whether they can articulate it or not. The more they think about it, the more adept they can be at avoiding fights. They might pass along some helpful tips.

Video Records

There's a lot to be gained by studying exactly how fights work, and who's doing what. We talked earlier about having kids walk through the fight, so that everyone can look for better options. The goal isn't mere punishment but to keep kids safe and make sure they make better choices.

Another source of information about fights is video from security footage. If the fight happened on school grounds, a record of the fight may be on your own cameras. The video may be a little blurry to use for reconstruction, but it can certainly be helpful for confirmation.

There may also be video from other kids. A lot of kids have cell phones, and kids can be amazingly stupid about what they'll film and post. There may be a record of the fight sitting on YouTube, and half the school will know where to find it.

If there's a fight, there may be ten kids looking on, and five kids capturing it on cell phones. You need to have a talk with all those kids, especially the ones crass enough to post video.

All of this—the positions of the players and any visual records—will make it easier to talk with parents. The kids, of course, may deny everything. The kid in the middle may stay silent in order to avoid a new beating. The more you know, the easier it will be to get to the bottom of things. Reconstruction will also help in getting other adults on board and in making sure that none of this happens again.

Neighborhood Rules

When it comes to fighting, of course you want the parents involved, and not just for obvious reasons. By fifth or sixth grade, the kids who fight tend to act out the rules of their neighborhood.

Now, this requires a shift in perspective since we're accustomed to looking at fighters as anti-social kids; but look closely. You'll find that fights often reflect the social values of the neighborhood.

If a neighborhood is all about money, the fighters will persecute the kid with shabby clothing. If adults in the neighborhood have contempt for heavy people, the kids will bully heavy kids. If the values of the neighborhood despise gay people, the ones who are picked on are the kids who are perceived as gay.

Consider what this means. This kind of fighting actually is *not* anti-social behavior. It's social behavior. These kids aren't rebelling as much as they're enforcing the social rules of the neighborhood. They are acting out values that their parents and other adults express under their breath when perhaps they think the kids aren't listening.

This is why you want adults on board and why you may have to be tactful about it. Parents may say quite truthfully that they have never told their kids to pick on kids who look different and that they never allow their kids to fight. But kids don't just listen to the nice messages: They listen to *all* the messages. You want the adults to be a united front to change this message.

Parental Involvement

Calling parents in over a school fight is often trying. The parents may be embarrassed. They may vigorously defend their child and refuse to listen to reason. It can help to have any neutral record speak for you: stepping through the fight, YouTube video, whatever is available.

Still, parents' denial can trump facts, and you want these parents to cooperate with you. Of course you can expel the kid anyway, but the best results come from adults working together to help kids learn from the experience.

Part of the problem is that if the kid is skilled at lying to you, he is usually even more skilled at lying to his parents. He's had more practice lying to them, and he knows their weak spots. If he tried shading the truth for you, he will do the same for them. However, he's entirely likely to tell a somewhat different story, since different lies will appeal.

Be prepared for the same tricks: appeals tailored to his parents' emotional weak points, memory drops, emotional distractions, and so on. Calmly take notes and point out any discrepancies. You want to model the behavior that dishonesty simply does not work.

This is still a kid, and the behavior is not yet hardened. You must send a clear message that fighting behavior needs to change; otherwise, even worse things may happen in the future.

Summing It Up:
High Points of Chapter Seven

The older kids get, the more dangerous fighting becomes. A fight between teenagers can bring the police. By middle school, it's crucial for kids to stop physically fighting and make better choices.

Stopping the Fight

Don't get in the middle. Nothing is served by you getting hurt. Follow your district guidelines.

Break their eye contact with each other. You can't get through if their eyes are magnetically locked on each other.

Repeat instructions. Flooding will interfere with their ability to hear, so keep it short and simple: "Back up, back up, back up."

Tap mirror neurons. Motion the students apart, and move the way you want them to move.

Consider an "honorable out" if you prevent a fight. A useful phrase is, "I would like to be mistaken. For a moment there, I thought…" Respect and disrespect are powerful social values, even the roughest neighborhoods.

Be the torero, not the bull. Breaking up a fight calls for finesse, not brute force.

Talking After a Fight

Your goal is to make sure the fight doesn't happen again. Discipline and guidance need to work towards that end.

Look for clues on what triggered the fight. Both you and the kids need to know the triggers in order to prevent similar fights in the future.

Honest apologies are a life skill and an excellent way to end a fight. Model an upright apology. Many kids have never seen a forthright, honest apology, and it may be a revelation.

continued ...

Finding the Truth

Remember that adrenaline magnifies. Not all exaggerations are deliberate lies.

Dishonest-looking body language actually may be fear or deference before authority.

Shading the truth—includes memory drops, emotions instead of facts, and appealing to your likes and dislikes.

Rather than accuse a kid of lying, say, "I'm afraid you're not taking this opportunity to put forward all the facts." Give the kid a chance to say something believable, even true.

Consider how kids have successfully lied to you in the past. This will show you how you may be vulnerable in the future.

"Reading" a Fight

Fear fighting can be remarkably destructive. Indicators include a kid not known for fighting, multiple attempts to avoid the fight, and astonishment on the part of the kid who did the damage.

To correct fear fighting, emphasize thinking through better options in advance and involving adults. Fairness will demand some punishment; however, there is little to gain by overly punishing a kid who acted from panic.

Circle fights offer insights into roles. The leader is at twelve o'clock: Turn him into a better leader. The henchman is at six o'clock: Watch out for this kid. Less invested followers tend to be at three and six. At one or eleven may be a kid who is trying to influence the leader, possibly to head off the fight. One of these kids may be the conscience of the group. Strengthen that kid's skills.

Neighborhood rules will determine who gets beat up. Ultimately, adults have a great deal to say about neighborhood rules.

Have clear goals with parents after a fight. Parents have to be involved, yet they may reflexively defend their child. Be specific when talking with parents, and have your notes in order.

CHAPTER EIGHT

Parents

Teachers and parents are natural allies, or at least they ought to be. The art of building kids into adults requires a team effort. The goal is for teachers and parents to work together smoothly and effectively.

This may require tact on the teacher's part. Any comment about one's child is sensitive. As one wise teacher put it, "Our children are our hearts. Criticize the child and you can inadvertently strike very deep." So we need to be mindful of the parent as well as the child, in order to build a solid alliance.

We'll work from three assumptions:

- The successful team doesn't fight among itself. Blaming each other goes nowhere. It destroys effectiveness.
- Every team has its strengths and weaknesses. Work with what you have.
- The effective team is consistent and confident. The corollary: Fear wrecks everything.

This chapter covers a broad range of issues around parents, from working with parents who may share your concerns to dealing with potentially violent parents.

Parents and Flooding

A stressed parent will have trouble with her own emotional regulation. The parent of a kid with behavioral issues is likely to be particularly stressed and probably has been for some time.

Even parents who have terrific kids can be stressed for many reasons. There are lots of single parents these days, some of whom are working two jobs. Some families are stressed from unemployment. Other parents may be highly successful but with jobs that are so demanding there's little time left for the children.

Under stress, flooding can hijack the best of us. It can leave parents acting in a bewildering fashion.

For instance, a mom and her son were checking out books from a library. The son's assignment was to write a paper based on references from books, not the Web.

The librarian couldn't let them check out books because they had overdue books on record. The mom went ballistic, screaming abuse as the librarian tried to explain. Finally, the mom started yelling, close to tears, "All right! All right! I'm a bad mom! I should have had him start this a week ago, it's due to tomorrow. I never should have let this slide. I get it! I'm a total failure as a mom."

The librarian was dumbfounded. She said, "I never meant anything like that. So he's got a paper to write, and he needs some references. Okay. We can't check books out, but he can work here."

Then the librarian sat them down with some books and helped them compile a bibliography using the sources at the library. The mom was near tears, she was so grateful.

Look at this in terms of flooding: Magnification and globalization abruptly took the mom to total failure. Then there were the "I" statements of anxiety: "*I* never should have let this slide. *I'm* a total failure."

There's also the rapid escalation and slightly manic mood swings of someone in the grip of flooding. Options disappear; problem-solving gets lost. At the moment it appears completely appropriate to launch a frontal attack on the local librarian.

Parents and Anxiety

The issue that anxious people suddenly talk about themselves explains a common problem that mystifies teachers. A parent is called in to discuss her son's behavior and promptly starts complaining about her job or her husband. Though she must be concerned about her son, she keeps talking about herself.

This is anxiety and flooding. Anxiety makes things all about "me." *My* husband, *my* problems, how overwhelmed *I* am. It's not that this parent doesn't think about her kid; her thoughts have been hijacked by anxiety.

Second, flooding causes problems with distraction and staying on topic. Third, flooding causes problems with impulse control, resulting in "over-sharing." Following an anxiety-filled situation, people are often mortified by the things that came out of their mouths.

Allies or Enemies

Teachers need parents to be allies. But if they are threatened, parents may see us as the enemy. When they are calm again, they can see us as allies again.

From the beginning, let the parent know you want this to be the best year yet for their child. Once parents know you want to the best for their child, they're far more likely to be responsive and work with you to make that happen.

As you work together as a team, remember that anxiety is specific and concrete. The parents are concerned about *their own* child, not the others. This is not the time to talk about the class as a whole or education in general. The focus needs to be their child and on reassuring the parents that their child is a priority.

Parents Under Pressure

Parents' ability to manage pressures and manage their own flooding will impact their ability to work with you successfully. Here are a few common pressure profiles:

Concerned parents. These parents may hit the occasional glitch, but they largely do a good job at managing their own pressures and bringing balance and stability to their kid. They tend to manage their own flooding well. They themselves are resilient enough to handle the occasional problem and help their child through. They're present enough to model caring, problem-solving, and resilience. Hopefully, every parent who crosses your path will be a concerned parent.

A concerned parent guides without overdoing control. After all, each child is a mystery in some way, with an unknown future. Wise parents, although they are certainly concerned, have the patience to let the mystery unfold while offering appropriate guidance and support along the way. But some concerned parents go too far.

Over-concerned parents, *aka* helicopter parents. Over-control speaks to anxiety. Fearing for their children's success at school, these parents do school projects for them. Consequently children fail to learn, which triggers more parental anxiety.

These parents readily become angry, particularly at you. They lack the resilience to handle imperfection, even a B+. And they model over-reaction to their children. We've already seen how fearful adults and over-control can escalate a situation.

The friend–parent. On the opposite side of the spectrum is a lack of parenting from parents who want to be friends with their children rather than parent them. After all, disciplining children is hard work and, at times, extremely stressful.

These parents have trouble with the stress of setting limits. They're doing what nearly everyone does: They're shying away from jobs that make them uncomfortable. You may feel these parents just need to be jolted into seeing the error of their ways, but if they can't manage their own anxiety, adding more pressure may not be the best approach.

The overachieving parent. During the first parent meeting for first grade, one parent asked, "Do you think my child will get into Harvard?" The teacher responded, "Please don't go there. Let's just enjoy first grade."

Overachieving parents tend to be hyper-competitive and may come from a fiercely competitive background. The Type A parent who drives his career through intense competition may not know how to cope if his child doesn't always "win." The dad screaming at his son's Little League coach is an example of misplaced and damaging pressure.

The child's success gets entangled with adult fears, which can produce real anger brimming over. The parent needs to contain her own flooding enough to leave breathing room for the child to develop, even though development involves the occasional mistake.

When this phenomenon shows itself in some cultures, it represents a different cultural norm. Some Asian cultures, for example, tend to see education as a series of difficulties and to believe that enduring difficulty is a way to develop virtue.

From that viewpoint, working hard, even suffering, is a valid growing experience. To be merely interested in or amused by learning is to never develop the key virtue of endurance and overcoming hardship.

Well, yes, endurance *is* a virtue. But parental pressure taken to the point where it undermines resilience is harmful.

Overtaxed parents. This might include single parents or parents with financial difficulties. Perhaps the parents are overwhelmed by the work involved in caring for their children, especially if one of the kids has special needs. Or perhaps one parent is sick or another child in the family is getting all the attention. As you learn more about what's happening at home, the behavior of this child may make more sense.

These parents may mean well, but they haven't been giving their kids enough one-on-one face time to meet their needs. These parents may be too tired to read to the child, hold the child on their lap, or simply stop and appreciate the child. Consequently, kids show up at school desperate for adult attention.

An overtaxed parent needs a short, practical list: The child needs to go to bed at a certain time every night and/or the homework gets done on a schedule. Keep it short, so this parent can experience success, even under trying conditions.

Keep these parent-types and issues in mind as you prepare for meeting parents. If you inadvertently trigger a parent's anxiety, things can escalate. Then nothing gets done. The better you manage inevitable tension, the more productive your meeting with a parent will be, and the more likely the parent is to co-operate with you.

The Parent–Teacher Conference

So let's look at how to use de-escalation skills in light of the parent–teacher conference.

You do not want your first contact with the parent to be negative. Hopefully, at the start of the year, you sent the parents a "welcome to the class" letter, so you have already established a positive footing.

The thoughtful teachers online at Teaching Heart have a smart tip: On meeting days, set up a waiting area outside your classroom with a table, chairs, and snacks. Have photos of class projects or other materials from class for the parents to look at while they wait. This keeps parents comfortable and interested as they wait, and starts things on a positive note.

Welcoming the Parent

Making parents feel welcome is an important ritual. Putting a guest at ease in an unfamiliar place is not just polite; it is also wise and productive. You're allies, building the bridge that joins you. That bridge is crucial to the child, so make it a strong and safe one.

At the first parent meeting, welcome the parent to your space. Do this the way you would welcome any guest: Stand up, walk over to them, extend your hand, and greet them by name. You might offer them coffee or tea or have snacks in your room.

Food is a universal peace offering, a way of smoothing tension. Friends and family eat together. Enemies do not. Offer parents something, even popcorn or a glass of cold water.

By the way, educators I've worked with report that food knocks 30% off the length of a meeting. It cuts tension and makes the work go smoothly. You have 15 minutes with these parents and, no doubt, a lot to cover. Have something available for them to snack on.

In keeping with making your guests feel welcome, start your discussion by saying something positive about the child. Then ask the parents to tell you some things their child does well or enjoys before you get into the hard stuff.

What You Said and What the Parent Heard

Let's say Mrs. Jones has come in to talk about her son, Billy. You show her the list of assignments, which is much longer than the list of what Billy has turned in. Mrs. Jones launches into a tirade that Billy does his homework, and she says that you always hated Billy anyway.

Of course, flooding has fueled magnification, but there's also a communication glitch. You said, "Billy hasn't done his homework." She heard, "You're a bad mother." Remember the ballistic mother at the library? Sometimes people believe they heard an insult even when none was intended. Then they fight over what they think they heard.

Make it easy for this mom to hear you correctly. Avoid the word *should*, as in, "You should set aside a time every evening," or "You should turn off the TV."

"You should…" generally translates to "You're stupid." This is an easy way to set off an argument.

The Violation Loop

As Mrs. Jones hears about the problem with Billy, she feels vulnerable. Defensive people are prone to attack. The pattern looks like this:

Vulnerability leads to violation. Once Mrs. Jones launches her complaints against you, you feel attacked and vulnerable, so you may be tempted to counterattack: "Maybe you don't understand me. If Billy doesn't start doing his homework, he'll flunk math." So now Mrs. Jones feels *more* vulnerable, and so she ups her attack and threatens to go to the school board.

This pattern doesn't read Vulnerability → Violation → Homework. Homework isn't on this chart. Neither is any other sort of progress.

The same pattern can happen without you. You tell Mrs. Jones about the homework. She promptly goes home, smacks Billy, and tells him he's lazy, like his useless father. Mrs. Jones felt vulnerable, so she attacked Billy.

Well, now Billy feels vulnerable and humiliated, so he'll search for a way to even the score. He might grudgingly plod through some homework for awhile, then act out by punching the smart kid in class. He feels vulnerable, so he takes it out on someone else. The cycle is still in motion.

Head Off Defensiveness

While you discuss the homework, tell Mrs. Jones that you know she's a caring mother. She came to this meeting because she cares about her kid. Lots of mothers have trouble over homework; she isn't the first.

Winston Churchill once observed that the fastest way to get someone to acquire a quality was to ascribe it to him. You don't need to argue with Mrs. Jones, you just need the homework.

Jargon and Paperwork

Avoid jargon as you talk with parents. The educational world is filled with acronyms, and speaking that way may be second nature for you. But flooding interferes with the language centers, and jargon becomes next to impossible for parents to understand.

In the same light, keep paperwork simple. If you give parents a complicated form, highlight in yellow what's most important. A form letter—say, for medical checks—may run two pages but only have two bits of crucial information, the vaccinations and deadline. Most parents' eyes glaze over when they see these forms, and then the school gets annoyed when they miss the deadline. Parents often say that they never even saw the form.

Work with the limits of the brain on overload: Highlight key information.

Military Families

By the way, if any of your students are from military families, be sure to use the authority signals we covered in Chapter 3. The upright posture, low voice, and direct gaze are basic to military standards.

It deeply annoys many military people to have to deal with civilians who are in positions of authority but don't know how to carry themselves. They find it insulting to have a civilian slouch, shrug, and expect to be taken seriously. They may tolerate it, but they often find it provoking.

You do not need to alienate a parent from the moment they walk in. Good body language will serve you with any parent, but it's a must around those in the military.

Some great step-by-step guides for teacher conferences are available on the Web, along with downloadable forms to help keep you and your students' parents organized. Details can be found in the appendix.

Resilience and the Family Story

As you work with parents to bring stability to their child, help the child calm down, and build a stronger foundation for the child, consider the role of resilience. Resilience, as we mentioned earlier, is a crucial life skill that helps children handle challenges and difficulties. Resilience plays a role in self-regulation. It's a key ability to succeed in school and in life itself.

You want parents to cultivate resilience in their youngsters. You also want to re-direct anxious parents from either overprotecting their kids or grinding them down. Some intriguing studies show that resilience can be developed by telling children the family story.

The studies come from Marshall Duke, a psychologist from Emory University. His wife, Sara, worked with children with learning disabilities and observed that resilient children seemed to know a lot about their families.

Well, our family stories convey a great deal of meaning about who we are and what we stand for. Children, to thrive, not only need safety; they also need meaning. And it helps for kids to know that they belong to something larger than themselves. Family stories accomplish this.

Working with Robyn Fivush, Duke developed a test for family knowledge. It included questions, say, on where their parents met or if they knew about something terrible that had happened to their family.

It turned out Sara Duke was right: the kids who knew the most about their families scored highest in resilience. In fact, knowledge of the family's story was also an excellent predictor of the child's happiness and feelings of well-being.

This study took place the summer of 2001. That September was the World Trade Center bombing. After this national trauma, the researchers tested the same kids again and found that the kids who knew the most about their families were best at handling the terrible news of 9/11.

Now, all families have narratives: some are success stories, some are tragedies, and some are mixed. The most resilient kids weren't from a perfect family. The most resilient kids knew the stories of both good times and bad, along with how the family managed.

For instance, let's say the family had a business, but it failed in the Great Depression. Or there were crop failures, or the homestead burned down. The cattle got trapped in a quagmire.

What did the family do? Who tried to get the cattle out? Who went into the fields for harvest? Who decided to move to the city, and why? Who did we leave behind? Where are our roots? What feels like home?

Ultimately, family stories gave kids the sense of being part of something larger than themselves. The most resilient kids saw themselves as part of their family's saga, and they knew the family could pull together and come back from reversals.

The stories also gave the kids the feeling that life makes sense. In the telling, family stories capture core values. Kids need to know these stories about character and overcoming obstacles.

You may be dealing with parents who are not highly educated or who are struggling with finances. But every family can tell its story. This simple thing can help parents build a critical strength that every child needs.

The Escalating Parent

Even though you do your best, some parents, unfortunately, may prove to be short-tempered. So while you should expect a positive meeting with parents, there may be times when a parent reacts badly from the start—and then escalates.

Many of the tips in this section come from Cathy Corl, a gifted social worker who worked with the Department of Child and Family Services (DCFS). The parents in her caseload were so angry or abusive the state had to take the kids away until they could learn better parenting skills. Corl is remarkable at de-escalating extreme parents.

Once a parent starts escalating, it can be tempting to get into a shouting match. This serves no one. It's not professional, and you're unlikely to get the results you want. As in any escalation, you need to keep your head. Try to stay a notch or two calmer than the parent at all times.

It will also help if you're correctly reading parents' cues. This starts with the body language we covered in the Chapter 3. As Corl points out, most parents with explosive tempers are not particularly skilled at conversation. Words are not their strong suit. That's why they bellow.

Another reason it is important to read cues is that you do not want to let the situation escalate to the point where things gets physical. You want a sense of the trajectory—whether the parent is heating up or cooling down. Recognizing the signs of flooding is invaluable: when language and thinking go off-kilter, agitation becomes palpable, and chemicals overtake the parent's self-control.

Corl tells the story of a parent who came in furious and started screaming at her. Active listening didn't work; the parent was flooding and couldn't hear her. Instead, the parent was getting himself more worked up.

Corl finally said, "Do you just want to scream at me or do you want me to try to help you? Because being screamed at turns off the part of my brain that can let me help you. I can't problem-solve here. What's your preference?"

That gave the parent a choice. This is important because flooding people typically feel that they have no choice. So the dad was able to stop and think: "Is there something I want, or am I just mad?" He had to sort it out, but it turned out there *was* something he wanted. He was able to make the choice of working with Corl, rather than just screaming.

As it turned out, this dad actually had a legitimate complaint underneath all the screaming, and Corl actually *could* help. But she would have never known for all that shouting.

Corl reported that the approach worked just as well over the phone. Sometimes the parent might be so upset he had to hang up a couple of times to pull himself together, but Corl would reiterate the same message: "I really think you have an issue I can help with, but I can't help under this kind of pressure. Please back that down."

When a parent is escalating, it helps if you can find something you agree on. Sometimes a volatile parent will rant about how the kids drive him crazy and his life sucks. Well, that's screaming at some *thing*, not you. That's not escalating towards a threat. So you can join in: "Yeah, life is tough." This is not someone who's going to disagree that life is tough. With that temper, life probably *is* tough. You have finally found something you can both agree on.

Productive Action

After you've taken the volume down a few notches, give this parent something productive to do. Try not to blame him. Blame will only alienate him, it won't help you, and it surely won't do the kid any good. Blame is ineffective. Your goal is results.

This parent has something that needs to be solved, like getting the kid to stop fighting. Of course, he doesn't want to look at the problem. Of course he gets angry and blames, rather than tackling the problem. Ever listen to talk radio? This parent is not the first person in America who lashes out bitterly when things don't go well. So don't blame him; blame won't help you help the parent, which in turn won't help your student.

Remind yourself that the purpose of an effective parent–teacher conference is to help your student. That will help keep you grounded.

Work in baby steps with this angry parent. You can tell, by volume alone, that this is not someone who has mastered problem-solving skills.

The first productive action is to get him to stop screaming. If he manages to stop yelling, genuinely thank him. He has done something new that required considerable effort. Acknowledge him for it. If you give this parent positive reinforcement, he is far more likely to restrain himself in the future. You want him to practice restraint, so reinforce it when you see it.

You want this parent to learn that if he dials it down, things get better. All his problems won't be solved, but for this brief moment spent talking with you, things feel better. He'll feel more in control. Besides, someone just said something nice to him; we all like a little encouragement.

This parent may only be able to talk with you for 10 minutes before he's overloaded and battling rage again. That's okay. If he's hit his limit, you can continue another day. It's far better that he experience 10 minutes of positive interaction, than the futility of 30 minutes of screaming.

Not in Front of the Kids

One nun was in charge of a group of fourth graders. A mom stormed in, furious because she felt that her child had been treated unfairly, that some other child got something that her child didn't get. The parent started to berate the teacher in front of the class.

The nun used a calm but deadly serious voice and asked the parent out into the hallway. There she said, "I understand you're angry, but you cannot talk to me that way in front of the class."

The mother listened to the teacher's point, agreed, and apologized. Then the mom went right back to chewing the nun out, but she kept it low enough the children couldn't hear.

The teacher thought this was an important step. She had established her rules and gotten the parent to agree. Then she could settle the complaint adult to adult. Adults have to "hammer it out" sometimes. The nun, although she didn't like it, could accept being yelled at: just not in front of her students.

"I Want to Talk to Your Boss!"

Teachers don't particularly like having parents threaten to go over their head, though it can be comforting to know your administration will back you up. Sometimes parents need to hear things confirmed by a higher authority. However, it's also true that your principal probably has enough to do and would prefer that you handle things without involving the administration, the district chair, and the school board.

When a parent demands, "I want to talk to your boss!" it's a sign this parent does not feel heard. She's searching for a new pair of ears to listen to her grievance.

These parents are usually visibly frustrated and flooding. They likely feel disrespected. They've made an "I" statement, so they may be at the anxiety stage on the escalation chart. This statement is about "me": "*I* feel disrespected," or "*I* am not going to put up with this." At this point, concrete issues with the student can be forgotten until the parent calms down.

You might also be feeling, "No one talks that way to *me!*" But consider once again: Do you want to be right, or do you want to be effective? It will be harder to achieve the desired outcome if you are at odds with the parent.

So stop. Breathe. Step outside yourself for a moment and consider ways to lower the tension.

The first way you could lower anxiety is to take all the anger out of your voice. Remember, the angry, belligerent voice isn't the strongest choice. The resonant voice of authority is best.

Consider the words the parent just said, along with the likelihood that she isn't feeling heard. Send out a trial balloon: "Mrs. Jones, am I missing something? Of course you can talk to the principal. You have every right to do that. But if you're saying something that I'm not really hearing, I want to attend to that."

Then square your body and listen with absolute attention.

Mrs. Jones may start, stop, or possibly burst into tears. She may start sputtering; perhaps people often don't listen to her, so it's hard for her to know what to say. Or she may start repeating the same things, over and over, as if she's trying to convince herself.

Listen to all of this. Attentive listening relieves anxiety. Then ask Mrs. Jones what she'd like to do. There is something you need to sort out about the child. What could be the first step in doing that? This gets you back to the problem.

A parent's roller coaster of emotions may leave you bewildered, but wild swings are not unusual with anxiety. Think of the last time *you* felt besieged by anxiety that was then suddenly relieved. You may have wanted to burst into tears yourself.

Assure Mrs. Jones that you can see how much she cares. Ask if she will agree to one small concrete step before she leaves the room. This is not the time to ask for sweeping changes, but one small step can help both of you get on track.

By the way, this protocol—stopping, affirming, and listening precisely—dramatically de-escalates arguments and lowers the likelihood of people going over your head. After all, if parents need to be heard, they might just as well be heard by you.

The Parent Who Walks Out

At the point a parent walks out of a meeting, it is probably too late to turn a meeting around. It is hardly wise to throw your body between the parent and the door. However, a parent walking out is not the sign of a successful meeting; the odds are slim that you'll get the cooperation you want and need.

Prevention is better than cure. First, know that this parent is flooding. Remember, adrenaline manifests in three ways: fight, flight, or freeze. Walking out is flight. It may be done with great dignity or high dungeon, but it's flight. She needs to get away from you.

This parent is probably so upset she doesn't know what to do. Her flooding levels have probably become unbearable. She certainly can't hear you, which is probably part of why things are going so badly. She's upset, frustrated, out of words, and probably at the limit of her self-regulation. In fact, walking out may be the best she can do. If you get between her and the door, she may do something she'll really regret.

Don't ever touch someone who's angry and trying to leave a room. Better to let her go cool off and talk with her later.

If you realize you've both hit your limits, consider the wisdom of abruptly switching gears. Stop, sit back, and calmly ask, "Are you getting a headache right now? Because my head feels like it's absolutely going to explode."

Her eyes may slide to one side and her mouth may drop slightly, as she stops and checks her head. She may nod. Just agree with her: "It's some business we're in, isn't it? Raising kids. I don't know how we live through it."

You have suddenly stopped fighting. You have suddenly made a connection. Adults everywhere feel bewildered and overwhelmed by raising children.

Take a moment. If this is as much as you can do that day, that's okay. If you have gone from fighting with the parent to bridging with her, you've made an important step.

Thank this parent for coming and give her a week or two to let things you've already said soak in. Even a momentary bridge is progress and something to build on the next time.

Potentially Violent Parents

It's one thing to handle a child physically lashing out at you. It's something else to handle violence from parents. Unfortunately, there are times we have to take these things into consideration. Sometimes a child's behavior issues were learned at home. This leaves you with a volatile parent as well as a volatile kid.

The rest of this chapter looks at what to do if a parent poses a physical threat. If you're a teacher, hopefully you will never have use for this section. The point is to keep you safe. You have every right to feel safe. Besides, if you're in a confrontation and don't feel safe, you're more likely to escalate along with the other person.

Be prudent, and in the future consider handling discussions by phone. There's no reason to get into a situation where your safety is at risk.

Cold Threats

Usually when we think of threatening behavior, we think of someone loud and hot-tempered. But in some cases the threatening person isn't emotional at all. In fact, they're cool, but distinctly threatening.

For instance, one parent had a series of conflicts with a teacher. He came up to her one day and said, "Do you own a light blue Chevy? License PL5 14?" She looked at him puzzled; he just smiled. Then she realized the implications. As the shock hit her face, he smiled more.

When someone goes to the trouble of seeking out your car and then lets you know about it, he means to frighten you. He's watching for your reaction. It gives him a sense of power. This person should be taken seriously, because this is a pattern typical of domestic violence. He may be accustomed to scaring people this way.

It's actually not your business at the moment to figure out if he's serious or not. What's important is that he immediately get it into his head that this is totally unacceptable.

Don't overthink this or get imaginative about what to do next. Even though this parent was smiling, turn the problem over to security. This person doesn't need a conversation with you. He needs immediate consequences.

This is really about power, so it's best not to show fear, anger, or righteous indignation. In fact, show no reaction at all. Say something neutral, like, "I'll be back in a minute," leave the room, and then return with security.

The least gratifying response to someone who is making a threat is uncurious, unimaginative, and bureaucratic: "You have to understand, we've had these situations before, and the administration has made it clear we need to hand these things to security. I'll let Jasper take it from here."

And let Jasper handle it, because he's six-foot-five and trained—and because no one knows what car he drives. You bow out of the picture. If you feel upset, go somewhere out of sight to be upset.

Do not get pulled into an apology or cat-and-mouse game. This is not in your interest. Make it as boring as possible. You can even explain in a bureaucratic way: "The paperwork is a pain, but you know, we have no way to telling these incidents apart. They all have to go into the same bin. We have our orders, and I don't have the authority to determine which ones should or shouldn't be reported."

Jasper, meanwhile, apart from filing a police report, will make it clear that this person is never to come near school grounds or make contact with you again. It may be tempting to escort him off the premises, but it's really much better to turn him over to the police.

Make sure there's a paper trail and get these things on file. Also file a record with your teacher's union so that if this parent threatens another teacher in the future, the union can support that teacher as well.

Safe Space

If you have to sit down with a volatile parent, don't schedule the meeting in a distant fourth floor annex after everyone else has gone home. Instead, meet in a room near the principal's office, at a time when there's a steady flow of people coming and going. Isolation could feel scary and might tempt aggressive people.

If possible, meet in a room of a reasonable size, with an intercom. Keep your cell phone easily accessible. Make sure the principal or assistant principal knows you're there, and arrange for them to back you up if needed.

You may want to have the principal, vice principal, another teacher, or even a union rep sit in with you. This third party's role is not to argue, but to be matter-of-fact and calm. If the parent is yelling and out of control, it's fine to call an end to the meeting. If the tone is truly threatening, you should not be alone in a room with that parent.

The Disembodied Voice

Child welfare workers often make use of the intercom as a way to de-escalate a parent. For instance, Cathy Corl, the gifted child welfare supervisor discussed previously, tells of regular incidents where a parent might be screaming, yelling, and escalating. Corl would call in on the intercom. Introducing herself, she would say, levelly, "If the tone doesn't change dramatically in the next two minutes, I will call the police. If this continues, I will need uniforms here. This is at my level of not okay."

The staffer would then turn to the parent, and calmly repeat, "That was my boss. And if the tone doesn't come down in two minutes, we'll have the police. I don't want to see that happen. Help me out here. Could you just take it down a little?"

The advantage of an intercom is that it's a disembodied voice. Remember: anger follows vision. A disembodied voice makes it harder to re-focus anger. You don't need the parent to start a new fight with administration. You just want her to calm down.

Oblique Phrasing

Note Corl's language over the intercom. It's not confrontational. In fact, it's both concrete and oblique: "If the tone doesn't change . . ." ". . . at my level of not okay." "We'll have the police . . ." There are clear limits and clear consequences, but it's more or less in the third person. The effect is very different from: "You there! Shut it!" A tone like that would only inflame things.

The goal is to shift the parent's thinking. I suspect the oblique phrasing cues a different part of the brain. The parent has to work a little to sort out what was said, and that brainwork distracts her from her anger or frustration.

The tone is criticized, not the person. It's entirely likely the angry parent isn't aware of her tone of voice. In fact, if she is seriously flooding, she may not quite remember what it was she just said. Not remembering what you just said is disconcerting, and the parent may take a moment or two to try to figure what she said that might bring the police.

The combination of oblique phrasing with clear standards seems to be extremely effective. The same combination was mentioned by staff from a number of child agencies that deal with extremely angry parents, many of whom have serious criminal convictions. The combination seems to cause the angry parent to recalibrate. Watch for the parent to pause, for her jaw to open slightly, and for her eyes to shift back and forth. She may look distracted, and her eyes may blink rapidly. She may re-start, slightly hesitant, in a different tone of voice. Give her time to do this. You want her to re-set and start over.

Now the teacher (or social worker) in the room does her part. She shifts away from confrontation and makes it a negotiation: "Help me out here. I don't want this to happen. Can we take it down a couple of notches?"

By the way, if the tone doesn't come down, your colleague will need to follow through and call the police. Never threaten without carrying things out. Each encounter you have with an aggressive person teaches her something—hopefully that she must deal with you in a reasonable manner. You don't want to teach her that the staff makes empty threats. That would actually reinforce the idea that it's okay for her to be out of control.

Eye Triangulation

Let's say the parent has been escalating, and you're starting to get concerned. For some reason you cannot find your back-up, and you have not yet left the room. Make sure there is some obstacle between you and this very angry person—a desk, several chairs, literally anything that will slow her down in case she does really lose it.

But let's say the parent abruptly shifts temperament. She's quieter; she's not exactly calm, but she looks preoccupied. Now you're doing the talking. She's kind of listening to you and kind of not.

Her eyes aren't glaring at you, but they're making brief, glancing darts in triangles: casually looking at you, then glancing to the desk, to the right of the desk and back to you. Or they're darting to the left of the desk and back to you. All the while, she's unexpectedly calm—and yet not.

That triangular glance is an "eye bounce." That means the person is estimating what it would take to get past the desk or the chairs and launch into you.

She does not look calm; she looks coiled. She abruptly stopped yelling because she's finished talking to you; she has now decided that it's time for action. Remember hostility, the last stage of escalation before violence: She has drawn a focus, and she is assessing exactly how to carry out a plan.

Stand up, keep talking, politely mention that you wanted to get something for her, and take yourself out of the room. In the future, deal with this parent by phone.

If nothing has happened, that's fine. Perhaps you were mistaken, and she simply has a facial tic. It's okay to err on the side of caution. You'd want your students to err on the side of caution, and what is good for them is good for you too.

Drunk and Belligerent

It may not happen often, but you may be in a conversation with a parent when you realize he's drunk or high. This is not going to be a particularly useful conversation. Even if it does go well, he might not remember what you talked about the following day. So you may as well close the conversation and try again later.

It's a bigger problem if the parent is drunk and belligerent. Someone drunk can be surprisingly changeable; he can go from spoiling for a fight to crying on your shoulder, or wringing your hand like his new best friend. Don't take any of this too seriously. People who are drunk can do mood swings.

If, however, he starts to get belligerent, you will need to take the situation seriously. Here's a tip: someone who is really drunk can't handle circles. Their eyes are blurred, they're none too steady, and the room, for them, may already be rocking. You will take all that unsteadiness and intensify it. No one who is seasick wants to fight.

For instance, talk with your hands, but moving in circles. Reverse direction now and again. Get his eyes tracking your hands. If he's high, he may be "strobing," or seeing "trails" behind moving objects. Walk in a half circle towards the door, or walk in circles around him. Of course, if he looks like he's going to fall over, stop. You don't need to take things that far. You just want to shift his attention to the queasy feeling in his stomach, rather having him take a swing at you.

It should be no surprise that a truly challenging child might have challenging parents. Keep in mind, the child did not get to choose her parents, and you do not get to choose the team.

It's for you as an educator to work with the parents as they are, and make the most of their strongest gift: the love they bear for their children.

Summing It Up:
High Points of Chapter Eight

Parents and teachers are natural allies, although it may not always seem to be. Tact and good planning will help you build a team.

Parents are disrupted by flooding, just as students are. Unfortunate parental behavior is often due to difficulty with managing discomfort.

The parent who keeps talking about herself is probably experiencing anxiety. Put her at ease as you steer the conversation back to the student.

Parents Under Pressure

Over-concerned parents are driven by anxiety. Work with these parents on anxiety control and the need to build resilience in their children.

Friend-parents have trouble with the stress of setting limits with their children. Acknowledge their distress, but enhance their skills for their children's sake.

Overachieving parents may be trying to teach their children virtue through hard work. Work with these parents on balance.

Overtaxed parents have too much to do and too few resources. Work with them in small, manageable steps so they can feel accomplished, rather than overwhelmed.

The Parent–Teacher Conference

Welcome the parents. They are guests in your space. Offer chairs where they can wait comfortably outside your classroom, with artwork from the children.

Snacks for waiting parents can be surprisingly soothing and may markedly improve cooperation.

Choose your words carefully when describing challenges. If the parent feels vulnerable or offended, she may take it out on either you or the child.

Avoid saying, "You should..." This readily translates to "You're stupid," and will be met with resistance.

Resilience

Resilience is one of the most important gifts any parent can offer a child. A simple way to build resilience is to have the parent share family stories with the child. Doing so helps children develop the feeling that they are part of something larger—a resilient family that is moving forward.

The Escalating Parent

Give the escalating parent a choice: do you want to yell, or is there something that you want? A useful phrase is, "Yelling turns off the part of my brain that can let me help you."

Genuinely thank parents for any positive step. If you want them to do more of some behavior—such as converse with you in a civil manner—thank them when they move in that direction. Even small shows of restraint may cost those parents considerable effort.

"I want to talk to your boss," is an indication that this parent does not feel heard. Take a breath, clear your head, and ask if you've missed something.

Potentially Violent Parents

Cold threats include "friendly" references that show knowledge of your car or your schedule. Show no interest or expression, get boringly bureaucratic, and turn the matter over to security or the police. If you're upset, don't let it show.

Meet the parent in a space near the principal's office if you have concerns about her temper. Have someone with you.

A disembodied voice from an intercom, using oblique language and clear consequences can help de-escalate storming parents.

Eye triangulation—the "eye bounce"—is a sign a parent may be about to lunge for you. Politely get out of the room.

If a parent is drunk and aggressive, use circles in talking with your hands. Get their eyes tracking your circles.

You are entitled to a safe work space. If a parent poses a threat, deal with her by phone, not in person.

CHAPTER NINE

Mental Health: When to Get Outside Help

The techniques we've covered so far should be helpful with most cases of school aggression that could escalate towards violence. But you may come across cases that are beyond the skills of ordinary staff and school counselors. These cases cross into the realm of mental health and require specialized outside professionals.

Mental health issues are widely misunderstood, and they generally have a great deal of stigma attached. This complicates the primary goals of getting help for the kid and having calm, productive behavior in your class.

Families have to be closely involved for children to make progress on mental health issues. Misunderstanding and stigma only add problems. The family may fight the very thought of outside help because of denial or shame. The family may turn inward, seeing outside professionals as the enemy and keeping potential help at bay. Meanwhile, inappropriate behavior erupts at school, kids increasingly reject the student who is acting out, learning doesn't happen, and negative consequences multiply.

We need to get past this logjam of misunderstanding and stigma in order to get the student the help she needs. If mental illness is involved, talking alone won't fix the behavior. More intensive treatment, possibly even medication, is needed to get at the underlying problem. This is a health care issue, and the student won't get better without better health care.

In this chapter we examine some of the issues around mental illness, especially ones that interfere with getting timely help. We then look at resources available to help educators handle mental health issues in a safe and productive way.

Mental Health in Kids

Mental health treatment isn't as simple as running a blood test and taking a pill. There are a lot of gray areas, and this is especially true for kids.

There's actually not a lot of difference between normative adolescent anger, angst, or depression and a condition that would qualify for a mental health diagnosis. The line blurs.

Moreover, mental health is a more fluid situation for kids. Kids change. Hormones shift, and kids may out grow some behaviors. Many diagnoses can't even be made until a child nearly reaches maturity.

So even if there is a mental health diagnosis for a kid, keep in mind that this might not be a lifelong condition. The key to improvement is timely and appropriate help.

It helps to consider mental health as one more form of health care. If a child had trouble with asthma, you wouldn't hesitate to direct her to the school nurse. You wouldn't wait until she was gasping and blue to get help.

As a teacher, you may be the first to notice mental health issues. The first step is directing the child to the school counselor. Whenever possible, keep notes on the behaviors that worry you so that you can refer to your notes when meeting with the counselor.

Early Signs of Mental Illness

One kindergarten teacher, Vera, told the story of a student we'll call Todd. Vera noticed something seriously wrong from the first day of school. Todd lashed out at other children with unusual vehemence for no apparent reason.

Vera began working with Todd's mother from the very first day. Vera had taught Todd's sister two years before and had a good relationship with the family. The sister had been a delight, and she knew these were loving parents. So when Vera witnessed Todd's disturbing behavior, alarm bells went off.

In their first meeting, Todd's mother maintained that he was "just a little boy" and "he'd grow out of it." Vera decided to send a note home with Todd each day to update his parents about his behavior.

After Todd had been in class about six weeks, his mother came into the classroom in tears. Her face was covered with deep scratches. Todd had been to a birthday party and had bitten another child very severely. When she tried to take Todd out of the playroom, he attacked her. The mother was still in denial and made excuses for Todd's attack on her: "He was over-stimulated. He was sorry afterwards."

Vera observed one of these apologies after Todd had physically hurt his mother. When his mother reprimanded him, he apologized, but it looked very insincere. He was watching from under his eyelashes to see how his mother responded. Although his mother believed he truly was sorry, he struck Vera as very manipulative; he seemed to have no real conscience.

At this point, Vera asked the mother to visit her family doctor and request a referral to a skilled child psychiatrist. The school had budget cuts, and this was beyond the work a school counselor could do. Child psychiatrists were rare in the area, and they faced a lengthy wait. The family doctor treated Mom's scratches and became a partner in their search for help.

A little while later, Todd's after school care provider, also a parent in the school, came to see her. Todd had been playing with her children's new kitten and had injured it. She also confided to Vera that Todd was interested in matches. She didn't know what to do because Todd's mother didn't seem to think there was a real issue.

Vera would never talk to one parent about another parent's child, but she took a file card and made a note of the date of the incident and the details. She assured the care provider that it was important for her to have come forward with this concern. Vera told her that if she ever again encountered a similar situation, she *must* report those behaviors not just to the parent of the child, but to a trusted authority who would follow up on it. After the care provider left the meeting, Vera called the social service authorities who needed to be involved.

After much discussion with Vera, Todd's mom realized that the problems were not "normal little boy" behaviors and that Vera's insistence on immediate professional intervention and support was not an overreaction.

It is important in a situation like this to keep extensive records that can be used to help the appropriate professionals understand the severity and frequency of troubled students' behaviors. It's hard for a busy classroom teacher to do that during class, so every day after the students left, Vera made notes. Those notes were very important in later conferences about Todd.

By the end of the year there was improvement in Todd's behavior, although it was unclear if he had begun to experience empathy. It took continual alertness and reinforcement to get him as far as restraining his aggression towards other children. He responded to positive reinforcement, but he particularly noticed when his favorite activities were taken away after aggressive behavior. Adults were alert for signs of harm and hopefully remained that way for a long time.

Serious Symptoms

The key symptoms that signaled an immediate need for professional intervention included:

Unusual aggression towards other children
Unusual harm towards a family member
Hurting animals
Interest in matches or setting fires

These are dangerous behaviors, and they signal the potential for worse to come. While it is true that kids grow out of some behaviors, it is not okay to just wait these out. Someone could get hurt in the meanwhile. And you do *not* want to delay, since these behaviors can become calcified.

It is actually rather typical that Todd's mother did not register a need for immediate intervention, even after she got hurt herself. At times it can be disorienting for people looking in from the outside to see how resolute the family can be at insisting that nothing's wrong. That resistance signals *more* of a need for professional help, rather than less. This parent is in denial and not able to do the parental job of seeking help for the child.

Now, if you recall the earlier case of Jimmy, who had raging tantrums, you might wonder why Todd's case should be considered so much more serious. Jimmy's behavior didn't involve trying to hurt children or animals. Jimmy genuinely liked other children and wished to make friends. Also, there were never any issues about fires or matches.

You do not want to wait until someone gets seriously hurt before you seek help for a child.

Diagnosis

The crucial part about seeking professional help is to address behavior. Diagnosis is a secondary concern. A child can be helped and behavior can change whether or not a formal diagnosis is ever identified.

Diagnosing mental health conditions in children is especially difficult. It's not uncommon for a student to have a string of different diagnoses. It's not necessarily that the child has a half-dozen emotional maladies; the child may well have some elusive condition that no one has quite figured out.

What's more, diagnoses are sometimes made for billing purposes. For instance, often there has to be a diagnosis in order for the psychologist or psychiatrist to get paid. Especially with kids, that diagnosis might be made before the professional has the chance to discover what's really going on so that the professional can get paid during the process.

A problem though is that kids can take a diagnosis very much to heart. Following a diagnosis some kids give up on themselves. They may see the diagnosis as some permanent stamp that there's something deeply, irrevocably wrong with them. Psychiatric labels have a lot of impact and can affect how a child sees himself for years.

Misdiagnosis

Another issue is misdiagnosis. One psychologist flatly told a 13-year-old, "You are bipolar with schizophrenic tendencies. You'll kill yourself or some other person by the time you're 18 or 20."

The kid shot back, "I'm an acid head. This is how we are."

Well, the kid was right; his problem was that he was doing too many drugs. Why the psychologist refused to consider the kid's own claim about drug use was a mystery. This kid eventually gave up drugs, went to Narcotics Anonymous, and became a functioning, successful adult.

While this kid wasn't personally crushed by the misdiagnosis, it certainly impacted his life. He decided that adults were idiots who wouldn't listen, brushed off help, and ended up being sent away to a boarding school.

There are many normal, functioning adults who were diagnosed with mental disorders as children. Be careful about these labels. Focus on behavior instead.

Don't Make Diagnoses

Do *not* attempt to diagnose a child yourself. Specialists having enough trouble making diagnoses; don't try your hand as a layperson. Labels on kids have a dangerous tendency to become destiny. The label isn't the important part of treatment; listening, talking, guiding behaviors, and appropriate medication are the most important issues for kids struggling with mental health.

Often we put labels on things because it makes us feel better. We feel more in control. If our work with a student isn't going well, we can tell ourselves it's because that student is _____.

When we fill in that blank, it's almost never something positive. We label the students who upset us. When we have positive interactions with students, we rarely feel compelled to label them. We call them by name and allow them the full, layered, surprising life-arc that we naturally grant to all growing kids.

By all means, if you suspect a kid is troubled, refer her to counseling. But in your work with the child, listen, talk, and focus on behaviors, rather than on labels.

If you really want to, you can label the behavior itself: This was a five-minute tantrum. That was fifteen minutes of cooperation. As an educator, you get to decide what behavior is acceptable in your classroom.

As in the example of Vera and Todd, stay in touch with parents and professionals and communicate the behavior you see in your class. Your class may be the only place where this kid doesn't wear a label, where she isn't prompted to live down to expectations.

Mental Health and Drug Use

An important benefit of early mental health care is that it limits susceptibility to drug use. Mental health issues can come up at the same time that drug use starts. Like the earlier story of the kid taking LSD, some drugs mimic or worsen the effect of mental illness.

Drugs, alcohol, and mental health issues readily combine and feed on one another. Mental health issues may emerge in preteens or teens about the time drugs and alcohol become more available. If there's stress at home or trauma in childhood, kids will look for some escape, and drugs and alcohol are waiting. Without legitimate treatment, kids may be tempted to self-medicate with whatever can be found on the street.

Kids with untreated ADD are also prone to self-medicate with drugs. A great many young people end up in prison because of drug use, when they actually need treatment for mental illness.

Addictions are much easier to prevent than they are to treat. Any sign of drug or alcohol use in middle school or earlier is particularly serious and needs to be brought before the school counselor.

The combination of mental health issues and chemical addiction is called a dual diagnosis: one diagnosis for mental health issues and one for an addiction. A dual diagnosis is a common complication for people who don't get timely help for mental health issues.

No individual needs this much trouble. It's in everyone's best interest that kids get the health care they need, at the time they need it—ideally *before* a crisis.

Older Students and Resistance

In the earlier case, troubling behavior was observed, but the child was too young to really engage in discussion. With older students it would be appropriate to discuss their behavior with them before bringing in professionals. But if mental illness is involved, those discussions may not go as planned.

Dr. Xavier Amador wrote an excellent book called, *I Am Not Sick, I Don't Need Help!* about winning cooperation from someone with mental illness. While the book primarily focuses on families, Amador's strategies can also be useful to teachers of older children.

Amador uses simple and insightful guidelines for gaining cooperation from someone with mental illness. I've paraphrased them here:

Listen respectfully. Basic respect often goes missing once mental health issues appear. Listen respectfully, even though you may not agree.

Empathize. Don't argue. Someone operating under a mental impairment believes their version of reality just as strongly as you believe yours. Find something you can agree on, if only that they feel the way they do.

Seriously consider their point of view, whatever it is. Then they are more likely to consider yours. If you postulate that, after all, you could be wrong, it makes it easier for them to consider that perhaps *they* could be wrong.

Partner and negotiate. Most people with mental health concerns retain a capacity for give and take. If they are treated fairly and their opinions are considered, basic elements of fairness can be tapped. You can use this to help them change problematic behavior.

A common sticking point is that someone with mental illness is apt to insist there's nothing wrong with them; the problem is all about someone else. It's easy to interpret this as pride, stubbornness, or just being a complete young jerk. Amador makes the case that instead there's a problem with brain function that has to do with insight.

With mental illness, arguing does not improve insight. But other strategies, like teaming up to do neutral experiments, *can* improve insight. And better insight can result in better behavior.

The Talk

The following story provides an example of how you might handle a conversation with a kid when there's a potential for mental health issues.

Let's say you teach sixth grade. You have Trina in detention, after she shoved another girl in class. You look over and she's glowering at you, not doing her work.

You ask, "Trina, why do you suppose you're here?"

Trina replies, "Because you hate me. All the teachers hate me. It doesn't matter what I do, you're going to give me detention. You're trying to get me thrown out of here."

Now in the past you might have told Trina to stop feeling sorry for herself, but you've begun to wonder if perhaps there isn't a mental health component to whatever is going on with the girl.

You notice a certain lack of insight, so you try a reality check.

You: "Well Trina, do you remember what happened just before I gave you detention?"

Trina: "That horrible little Julie shoved me."

You: (Consider her observation, and acknowledge that you could be wrong.) "Now, perhaps I'm mistaken, but I was standing right there. From what I saw, you shoved Julie."

Trina: "She shoved me in the stomach."

You: "Did you actually see her hand come towards you and push you?"

Trina: "No, she doesn't need her hands. She does it with her mind."

You explore this for a while and it's clear that yes, Trina really does think that Julie can shove her with her mind. According to Amador, you might consider this as a hypothesis, and find a way to test it.

You: "Well, why don't we try an experiment? Let's say we're both scientists. Now, I say you get detention because you shove kids, and you say all the teachers will give you detention anyway. And Julie's in the mix.

So why don't we test that? What if you tried going a few days without shoving anybody? Just do something else. Ignore Julie and leave your hands in your pockets.

We could try that for a few days, and then meet back here and look at the results."

Someone with a complete lack of insight would find this experiment appealing, if only to prove you wrong. Trina would be convinced she will get detention anyway, just as you are convinced if she stopped shoving kids she could stop getting in so much trouble. You both might gain some useful information along the way.

What's Normal?

You can see from Trina's story how it can be hard to tell which situations reflect ordinary adolescent anger and which ones involve serious mental health issues. A *lot* of kids have a complete lack of insight when it comes to anger. Now, shoving with the mind is not exactly an everyday event, but for all you know, her parents are getting a divorce and that's why she feels like she's getting shoved around. And why she needs to shove back.

On one hand, Trina's behaviors are not dangerous like Todd's were. But if she's truly having tactile delusions—truly believing someone can physically shove her using mental powers—then she needs professional care and probably medication. And the sooner she gets help, the better off she'll be. This should not be put off.

Whatever's going on, Trina's behavior and comments show that this is more than a layperson can manage. Her teacher must talk to the parents and turn the situation over to professionals.

The following sections discuss additional resources that can help you, as an educator, to understand and work effectively with students who may be struggling with mental illness.

The National Alliance on Mental Illness (NAMI)

NAMI—the National Alliance on Mental Illness—is an excellent resource for educators, parents, and even for students themselves. NAMI is an advocacy and support group for individuals and families concerned with mental illness. There are over 1,100 local chapters across the United States and Canada. If you can't find a branch near you, the organization has excellent online resources.

NAMI chapters are often staffed by volunteers affected by mental illness. Some NAMI members and workers have family members struggling with mental health issues. Other members have mental health diagnoses themselves. Last but not least, many NAMI members are mental health professionals.

Through NAMI, you might find presenters to come out and speak at your school, conduct an in-service, or help educate your students on issues of mental health in age-appropriate ways. You can also learn more about care options that are available in your community.

NAMI is not a mental health center. It's not a replacement for medical treatment. But it is a great resource for learning more about mental health issues and replacing myth with facts and current research. NAMI provides various types of support for families affected by mental illness, including sharing information about treatment options available in the community.

NAMI programs

Another excellent initiative from NAMI is a catalog of programs for young people and teachers. It's called, *Innovative Programs Targeting Youth and Young Adults Living with Mental Illness and their Families.* It's a compendium of dozens of programs developed by member groups, specifically with young people in mind.

This catalog has a broad range of resources for teachers, parents, siblings, family members, and school groups. They have some very interesting programs, including a workshop for teachers on spotting early symptoms of mental health issues in children and another workshop on working with kids with mental health issues. Some programs even offer continuing education credits.

There are materials for support groups—such as student groups, parent groups, and sibling groups. NAMI also provides information about a broad variety of mental health topics. The materials NAMI provides use accessible language, and information for children is age-appropriate

All programs may not be available at every location. However, you can get contact information to track down different programs. Program creators are often willing to share their materials.

The catalog is available as a free download; the link is listed in the appendix. Check for periodic updates. NAMI member groups are continually developing and refining new material. If there's a problem that concerns you, it's very likely that one of the NAMI member chapters has already worked on it. Make the most of their hard work.

Crisis Intervention Teams (CIT)

The police do not always have a stellar reputation for managing mental health calls. Some educators or families hesitate to call in the police, because they are afraid of what the police might do. Crisis Intervention Teams (CITs) are designed with exactly that fear in mind. CIT is a broad initiative to train police in the skills they need in order to manage mental health calls safely.

As mentioned earlier, the CIT movement started in Memphis, when an emergency call went badly and the police shot and killed a person with mental illness. After the subsequent investigation, the police and mental health community worked together to find a better way. The five-stage escalation scale is just one outcome from that work.

The goal of CIT is to train police in specialized skills to manage mental health calls safely, skillfully, and with dignity. The exciting thing is that it works.

Gifted Cops

I was able to spend a good deal of time observing and studying the Chicago CIT trainings, which were the brainchild of Lieutenant Jeff Murphy (now retired). Lt. Murphy was one of those people with a natural gift for de-escalation, the cop equivalent of a kid whisperer. He would talk about his early days on the force, when his precinct would get a call about a regular they called "Tiny." Tiny was a good 300 pounds, he had mental health issues, and he would periodically go off his meds. Bringing him down typically required every free officer on the shift.

As a young cop on his first call with Tiny, Lt. Murphy was climbing up rickety stairs with a bunch of officers when Tiny started tossing cops in all directions. When Tiny came to Murphy, he stopped, looked down at him, and said, "You, I like." And Murphy got to bring him in.

The desk sergeant, having seen enough of his officers thrown down stairs by Tiny, started dispatching Murphy to cover the calls. Murphy would hike up the stairs and say, "Aw, Tiny. Whaddaya doing?" And Tiny would come along willingly to the hospital.

Much later, Lt. Murphy developed the CIT training for Chicago, and convinced the department to train two officers from every precinct. After all, it's not enough to have people trained. There have to be enough trained people in enough places that they can actually be available when needed.

Desk sergeants would watch for the officers who were best at de-escalation, and encourage them to take the training. The upshot was that many of the most gifted officers in the city were funneled to this project. Some of them were astonishingly good.

In Chicago, part of the training consisted of role-plays that used specially trained actors with their own history of mental illness. This made the training quite authentic and more than a little demanding. The role-plays were filmed, so we could later run the tape and study precisely what had happened. After the most impressive sessions, I would sit down with the officers and actors and debrief: "All right.

At this moment something changed. What happened? What were you thinking?" It was a wonderful opportunity.

Various forms of CIT training are available around the country. You can find links in the appendix to find guidelines on how to get CIT in your community, if it is not already there.

Get Acquainted

If your police force already has a CIT, it may help your peace of mind to actually meet them. Understanding how a crisis will be handled may help you feel more confident calling the police if you need to. After you've talked with CIT officers, heard their stories, and had an opportunity to listen to the team answer questions, you may feel more confident about calling them in.

You might set up a meet-and-greet through a NAMI event or possibly through a Community Action Policing (CAP) program. Or you can invite the CIT to speak at a professional development event for your district. If these programs exist in your area, request a session with a CIT. You will learn a lot from their stories.

If possible, find out the best way to directly request a CIT. Otherwise, if you have to call 911, the dispatcher may be tempted to send whichever officers happen to be closest. There may be a specific way to request the CIT.

Ask how to recognize the CIT if they're on the call. For instance, Chicago CIT has a service badge worn by all team members, but the writing is tiny and impossible to read if you're flooding. It's helpful to know what to look for.

Courts and Treatment

The CIT model is designed to work hand-in-hand with enlightened courts. Mentally ill students will not get better in jail. They need treatment and probably medication.

Of course, the CIT are trained to talk people down and to contain them with as little force as possible. Then they follow protocols as to where, exactly, they should take individuals to get them the treatment they need.

The system coordinates with mental health facilities that are prepared to take in clients on short notice and with the courts who can route people with mental illness to treatment rather than to jail.

Since the school shootings in Newtown, Connecticut, more mental health funding has been made available around the country. You want this coordinated approach in your community. Again, reach out to your local NAMI chapter for more information.

Prevention of Violence

In potentially volatile situations that involve mental illness, we need to think in terms of prevention. In Newtown and in many similar cases the escalating person had gone through anxiety, past anger, and into hostility, which included identifying a target and preparing the means of attack. Only then did they cross into violence.

Because many violent individuals are reclusive, all this escalation may happen without anyone outside of the family noticing. The family itself may be in denial. Yet there are other cases of school violence that were averted specifically because an educator *did* notice and acted effectively.

We saw a similar pattern in mental health facilities preceding a resident's violent break. The resident might have been escalating up the chart without anyone noticing. In other cases, one or two staffers had noticed but only mentioned the situation to their friends on the shift. They might have had a word with the charge nurse, but beyond that, they hadn't known what to do. Any concerns should have been report-ed and addressed immediately. Instead, the staff had just mentioned it to their friends.

Without a clear next step, it's easy to do nothing. Then, as a situ-ation is accelerating, it's hard to think clearly. It's better to become familiar with options and services ahead of time. Then, if you need to, you'll be able to create a safe plan that includes skilled professionals who can intervene and get the individual the help she needs—and keep the community safe in the process.

Summing It Up:
High Points of Chapter Nine

Mental health services are a form of health care. You wouldn't wait until a child was in crisis to make other health referrals; likewise, you should not wait for a crisis when mental health issues are involved. As a teacher, you may be the first to notice signs that a child needs help.

Fear and stigma are issues that commonly keep kids from getting the mental health care they need.

Early intervention matters. Do not wait until a student's troubling behavior becomes calcified. Some forms of mental illness get much worse if left untreated.

Drug and alcohol addictions are common complications of untreated mental health issues.

Don't diagnose. Diagnosis in children is difficult at best. Misdiagnosis does active harm. Focus on behaviors rather than labels.

In younger children, signs of mental health issues include harming others—children, family members, or animals—and taking an undue interest in fire or matches.

In talking to an older child who may have mental health concerns, be respectful, seriously consider the student's point of view, and propose a neutral reality test. The more you listen to a kid with mental health issues, the more likely it is the kid will listen to you.

Mental health issues cause problems with insight. What may seem obvious to you may seem absurd to somebody suffering with mental illness.

Prevention of violence must be the primary goal when mental health issues appear to be escalating towards aggression. Often adults working with the child notice dangerous developments but only mention them to their immediate circles. Instead, bring your concerns to appropriate professionals. Get that kid help.

continued ...

Outside Resources

NAMI, the National Alliance for Mental Illness. NAMI is a non-profit that educates and advocates around mental health issues. It's a great resource for educators, families, or students.

Crisis Intervention Teams are police who have been specially trained to answer mental health calls with skill and dignity. You want this training for your community law enforcement.

Special mental health courts often work with CIT teams to route people with mental illness away from jail and toward the treatment they need.

Newtown and Beyond

This chapter primarily examines mass shootings. In high-crime neighborhoods, school shootings have largely been deterred by using metal detectors. But Newtown-style, planned, suicidal mass attacks, occurring in areas unprepared for violence, present a new and difficult set of problems.

In looking for solutions, we'll revisit many of the themes of this book. The focus of this book is prevention: de-escalating situations *before* they become crises. A mass shooting is the very definition of a crisis. The safest way we can protect children is to keep the crisis from happening at all.

This chapter looks closely at a number of shootings, including planned shootings that were prevented entirely, and it presents ways we can protect the children in our charge. There is a small section on what to do at the moment of a shooting, but at that point the harm has already happened. Our real goal is to keep things from going that far.

So, while this chapter discusses some disturbing events, keep your eye on the larger goal: finding ways to prevent violence. We will look at mistakes people made so that we can be sure not to make the same mistakes in the future. We'll also look at what people did right—but not only heroics under fire. We'll look at ordinary people who happened to notice a single odd thing that saved lives. After looking at these situations, we will have strategies that we can use to avert mass shootings or to deal with them—things we must notice and things we can do.

There are certain things we won't cover. We'll have less to say about de-escalation, since that isn't an option under automatic fire. However, if there is time to talk, de-escalation skills may be used to great effect. We'll look at such a case in depth.

We won't cover political issues, like arming teachers in schools or gun control. Both sides of these debates have covered the arguments at length, and there's little to be gained by rehashing them here. We'll put politics aside and focus on practical solutions.

After the Newtown shootings, grieving families formed the Sandy Hook Promise. The information in this chapter is offered in the spirit of their efforts: "To be open to all possibilities. There is no agenda other than to make our community and our nation a safer, better place."

National Response to Crisis

The Newtown tragedy was not the first time the United States has been shocked into action by the massive loss of life at a school. I don't mean the Columbine shootings, but the Our Lady of Angels fire.

In 1958, fire swept through a two-story Catholic grade school, killing 92 children and 3 nuns. Most of the deaths came from just a few classrooms, which had turned into lethal traps.

The school had passed a fire inspection a few weeks before. But after the fire, investigators found a long list of problems, from structural issues to a lack of fire doors. Many of the safety basics we now take for granted, from sprinklers to automatic alarms, were not present because they were not required in older buildings. Other basics were present but misplaced, like fire extinguishers that were kept seven feet off the ground.

Each problem had a rational reason. For instance, although the school was brick—required in Chicago, which had already burned down once—it had a wooden interior. The wooden interior was lovingly polished with wax that proved to be highly flammable.

These problems were not a product of neglect. Nuns showed great courage in protecting the children, but some of them didn't know what to do. Once the fire exploded, firemen and police flashed to the scene, but the fire was faster yet.

All of the adults involved, from nuns to administration, from the fire department to the police, were responsible, reasonably intelligent people. But no one had put together the pieces or considered the consequences should something go wrong. For instance, they all would have agreed that sprinklers were good, but retrofitting an old building was decided to be too costly.

There's another important point: the fire was so deadly because it had escaped notice for so long. It had smoldered for at least half an hour in a trash bin before it exploded up the stairs. Had anyone noticed that the trash was smoking, there would have been ample time to put the fire out or evacuate the building. There had been a window of opportunity during which the fire could have been stopped, but it had passed unseen.

Our national standards in fire regulations date from that tragedy. Many children are alive now because of changes that were made in the wake of that fire. We couldn't bring back those kids, but we could make sure there weren't more fires like that one. Adults around the nation pitched in together and committed to do better. Meetings were held everywhere; practical changes were made. In the over 50 years since the fire, we have not had a fire like the one at Our Lady of Angels.

Victims, Villains, and Heroes

Our reaction to Newtown isn't working that way. No one expects we'll go another 50 years without another mass shooting.

For the moment, let's not go into who's wrong, who's right, or who's to blame for the impasse. We don't need to talk about the changes in America between 1958 and 2013. But I will point out we are not substantively more stupid now or more inadequate as a people. In fact, we have tools now that we didn't have then. We're smart, but we need to take some pointers from 1958.

A crucial difference is that we in the present have been waylaid by a toxic pattern in our public discourse. The formal name of the pattern is "victims, villains, and heroes," and you can read more about it elsewhere. In short, it's a turbo-charged pattern of blame, vitriol, and recriminations. It's extreme and exhausting, and for all the effort expended, it delivers astonishingly poor results. This pattern was intentionally avoided in 1958. However, since Newtown, volatile, divisive arguments have consistently paralyzed practical action.

The other thing about this pattern is that practical voices lose the floor to extremists. There may be common sense solutions, but they get drowned out by the noise. This is why we are not going to touch any of the political questions. This pattern is so volatile and so toxic that it makes the search for solutions all but impossible.

Now, there are guidelines to avoid this breakdown, and we're going to follow them here. One guideline is to find a practical thing to do, and go do it. In 1958 the country didn't get embroiled in finger-pointing and in-fighting. They found practical things to do, and then they did them. There was a laundry list of things that had gone wrong at Our Lady of Angels. If you were looking for things that could be improved, it was a target-rich environment.

In our present situation with gun violence, there may not be a perfect solution for shootings. But then we still don't have a perfect solution to school fires, either. Instead we have some very good solutions that have made an enormous difference. Remember, there has not been a school fire as destructive as Our Lady of Angels since that time. We can approach the issue of school violence in a similar way—by identifying things we *can* do—and we can begin by looking at school attacks that were prevented.

Smoke Detectors

Alert Kids

Recently a teen in Oregon started walking up to classmates and initiating odd conversations. He cheerfully talked about how he could make bombs and showed off his copy of the *Anarchists' Cookbook*. It was all rather unsettling. Other kids didn't know if he was joking or not.

One student decided the situation felt wrong. Whether or not the first boy was joking, this second kid decided he didn't feel safe and that school was supposed to be a safe place. This second teen told his mother, and his mother discussed the first boy's comments with a friend in law enforcement. A day or so later the story made the news, as the bomb squad in hazmat suits carted off six homemade bombs and a detailed plan for a Columbine-style massacre.

The final stage before violence is hostility: a threat, a specific target, and the means to carry out the threat. This kid had acquired the means and escalated almost to violence without anyone noticing. A single person who *did* notice made the critical difference.

In cases like this there's often oblique aggression. The kid doesn't sound angry; in fact, he sounds pleased and eager to share. He says, "Wouldn't it be cool to be up in the cafeteria with a Bushmaster? You could jam the door, and take out half the school. Cool!"

He's talking to kids who would be on the dead list. They're supposed to laugh, and they often do. He's gaming them.

This kind of talk is designed to unsettle people. It's a mixed message: friendly but vicious. Mixed messages are *more* disturbing than overt threats. Meanwhile, the aggressor watches other kids trying to laugh it off but looking uneasy. And he likes that they're uneasy and ignorant. He likes the power it gives him.

Whether or not this kid has an arsenal under the floorboards, students shouldn't be subjected to this harassment. It's rather on a par with the creepy kid who sidles up to girls, says inappropriate things, and then laughs it off: Just kidding. Well, the girls are there for school, not creepy games. They shouldn't have to put up with harassment, and if they go to their teacher or school administration, their concerns ought to be addressed. Kids need to know their concerns about veiled threats will be taken seriously as well.

In other forms of violence, the threatening behavior would be considered grooming. Predators often float a trial balloon. They test what they can get away with. When it comes to school shootings, they need to discover that they can't get away with anything at all—no vicious/joking comments, no games, no threats.

The kid sharing his violent vision for the school is testing his ability to intimidate. The sensible approach is to call an immediate stop to the behavior. Notify the law, have his room searched, and have his computer taken away and examined. If nothing turns up, that's great. Send the kid to counseling and see what on earth is causing him to make such creepy threats. But in many cases, something deadly *is* found, and a potential crisis is averted.

It's easy to fool kids with mixed messages. So, in order for kids to be alert to a veiled threat, they must be taught to listen to their gut feelings: Do I feel safe? Why are my alarms going off? The results of their self-questioning may be somewhat murky. The alert may register in a section in the right brain that isn't particularly articulate. So it's okay if this feeling of alarm isn't easy to put into words.

As the adult, listen carefully even if the kids are inarticulate. Be patient. Don't discount the issue even if kids struggle to pinpoint just what feels so wrong. Give the kids time to recount specific words, behaviors, and facial cues, like the other kid's face lighting up when he talked about shooting people. That's a cue that sends a message, and it's appropriate to heed it.

Kids often talk. This is not al Qaeda. The Columbine murderers talked and even posted things on Facebook. As in the Oregon case, alert kids—those who are listening and alert to their feelings—can prevent aggression from going further.

Alert Teachers

A recent shooting at Santa Monica College involved a young man, aged 23. He had come to the attention of authorities while in high school, when an alert teacher noticed he was researching automatic rifles online. They searched his room and found explosives. He went into a psychiatric hospital.

A few years later he was living back at home with family. But somewhere along the line, people stopped being alert. In a pattern not unlike Newtown, intelligent family members became strangely obtuse about danger building in their own home.

The shooter had begun manufacturing his own weapons, evidently in his room. After the attack, the police found two homemade zip guns and a home-assembled automatic rifle. Clearly he had been at this for a while. Assembling the automatic rifle required a drill press, not a small piece of equipment. He had also purchased an enormous amount of ammunition.

It's hard to know what the family was thinking. In what's become a familiar pattern, he killed his family members first.

Now, there is a peculiar point about this shooting. Once he left home, the young man fired at people on his way to the college. He shot one driver, then a woman at the college at point-blank range. Another person was killed when the driver's car crashed. But otherwise he shot and missed.

For instance, he opened fire on a bus, and people were hit by flying glass but not by bullets. At the college, students took shelter in a safe room; he fired at the safe room, but no one was hit. He also fired on the police when they arrived; they returned fire and killed him.

Now, the police felt that Santa Monica was just very lucky that day, and it certainly was. The police reported there was nothing wrong with the home-assembled rifle. It was unclear if the shooter had ever practiced with it, but even experienced shooters can fire and miss.

However, shooting is a skill; it's not just luck. Perhaps the family didn't adequately monitor the son, but (unlike the family in Newtown) they don't appear to have taken him out for target practice.

The family's lack of awareness cost them their lives. But their lack of active support may have helped prevent further harm to the community.

The teacher in the young man's high school had done the right thing years before and prevented trouble. Later, the family dropped the baton. As we see in so many cases, follow-up is crucial. And it's especially critical that the family remain alert and involved.

Alert Community

Sometimes the person who notices something wrong is an unrelated stranger. And that one person may not know what to do.

James Holmes was the college student who killed 12 and injured 58 by shooting into a crowded theatre in Aurora, Colorado. The alert person who noticed trouble brewing was the owner of a local shooting range where Holmes wished to practice. The owner called the number Holmes had left and heard a phone message so disjointed and bizarre that he left word with his staff that Holmes was not to be admitted but was to be sent directly to the owner if he ever showed up.

This man's actions are similar to the pattern Zak Mucha and I noticed in our work at psychiatric facilities. Sometimes staff noticed something was wrong and told their immediate circle of colleagues. But beyond that, their responsibility was unclear, so they did nothing further.

There's a slogan for abandoned packages on trains: "If you *see* something, *say* something." The great majority of times, the package is harmless, perhaps nothing more than old laundry. And that's fine. But if something strikes you as dangerously amiss, troubling enough that you discuss it with your friends, then you should also discuss it with someone in law enforcement. Let a professional check it out.

Computers

Some shooters, being mentally ill and reclusive, rarely talk and may have little interaction with anyone, including their own families. But they tell their computers everything.

Mass shootings tend to involve long hours of meticulous, even obsessive planning. It was reported that Adam Lansky, the Newtown shooter, had detailed data on mass murders in a spreadsheet so extensive that it must have taken hundreds of hours to compile. His family may not have known about it, but his computer did.

The kid making bombs in Oregon did his research on the Internet. The shooter in Santa Monica assembled his arsenal via his computer. All of this took a long time, and each shooter's computer was his silent accomplice.

With the proper technology, computers can be set to sound an alert under designated conditions. The software would need to be along the lines of parental controls that already exist, but the goal is entirely manageable: Have the computer report obsessive, dangerous searches, or use web-based tracking, similar to the way search companies track your shopping preferences. Make it hack-proof and simple for parents. The same technology could be implanted in school or library computers, which are the other places kids have been known to prepare school attacks.

Remember, we're not talking about casual curiosity in a news item, but focused, obsessive behavior.

Now, before you get concerned about privacy, consider: Lansky of Newtown, the Oregon bomb-maker, and the Santa Monica shooter were all young people, living at home. These computers were bought with their parents' money, because these young people were either not old enough or not functional enough to hold down jobs and live on their own.

The parents—who were most at risk, but paying the bills—missed signals that later proved fatal. Meanwhile, the computers knew everything. The outcomes could have been very different if the computers had been programmed to flag the parents or the kids' doctors.

Safer Buildings

Now we'll look at some of the physical safety measures being put in place for schools.

Substations

An interesting development in Minnesota is that communities are placing police substations on or near school campuses. This is different from increasing armed patrols at schools. The problem of putting police in schools is that police are accustomed to dealing with adults, and mouthy youngsters might end up in handcuffs.

The police at a substation aren't guards; they just go about their business. In some sense the school becomes similar to the diner that offers coffee and donuts to the local cops. The cops go in and out on an irregular basis, and their presence acts as a working deterrent.

Mass shooters tend to seek out places where they can do a great deal of damage uninterrupted. Now, having police stations near schools doesn't change the overall problem of mass shooters. Instead of targeting a school, they might target a shopping mall. But I think most of us can agree that if we're going to protect any place, we should start with schools.

Shelter

Safe rooms work. Safe rooms protected the Santa Monica students. The kids heard gunfire and knew where to go.

A common, easy-to-implement change is that classroom door handles can be refitted to ensure that doors can be locked easily and quickly by the teacher or closest student.

Given the increased danger if a shooter gets inside a school, funding is becoming available to improve perimeter security to keep the shooter out. This strategy requires re-thinking one long-time characteristic of schools—their openness, exemplified by easy access, visibility, and open spaces. Most schools have a lot of glass and a lot of entrances.

Though you may not have noticed it, some grade schools in North America are already equipped to withstand automatic weapons. Some Jewish schools are surrounded by high brick walls, with a central gate and no direct line of fire. Schools for the very wealthy or diplomats' kids may exist in a high rise, with a secure lobby and elevator access that can be cut off in a time of danger. So solutions exist, even though these schools are different from what we normally expect in this part of the world.

Other technologies are being worked out, say, to trap a shooter within a building. This would involve automatically sealing fire doors to contain the threat.

Talking Down an Armed Intruder

Obsessive mass shooters may enter firing, but all armed intruders aren't the same. Some pause to talk, and that provides an opening.

Michael Hill, of Decatur, Georgia, had a previous history of threatening incidents, and a diagnosis of bipolar disorder. About a month before this situation, he appeared in court for threatening actions and was given parole. For whatever reason, he was directed to anger management, not medical treatment.

At the time of this incident, Hill had acquired an automatic rifle and went to an elementary school. He was buzzed into the building when he followed a legitimate visitor through the entry. Hill stepped into the school office, gun drawn, where he encountered Antoinette Tuff, the bookkeeper. Hill's first response was not to shoot, but to announce, "This is not a joke!" But by dint of not shooting, it was possible to talk.

Tuff, as it turns out, had the instincts of a first-rate hostage negotiator. She provides a note-perfect lesson in how to de-escalate someone with a weapon, including someone with mental health issues.

Tuff stayed outwardly calm, though she was inwardly terrified. She obeyed non-violent orders, like making a call to the local TV station or putting a message on the school's PA system. She talked with the gunman as she did this, buying time and recovering from the shock. Yet if Hill tried to do something potentially violent, like going down the hall towards children, Tuff stepped in and dissuaded him.

The bookkeeper asked Hill about himself. When at first he didn't answer, she told him about her own challenges in life, becoming a real, three-dimensional person and building a personal connection.

Eventually Tuff got him talking. As Hill described his feelings of hopelessness, she found herself thinking of her own child with multiple handicaps. Tuff was able to empathize. Since she could see the inner man, it was easier to bridge to him.

Tuff didn't argue, but every time Hill insisted that his life was over, Tuff said he still had a chance. He hadn't hurt anyone yet; they could all recover from this. He still had a future. And she was alert when things agitated him, like people moving outside the office. As he escalated, she calmed him down. She anchored herself at a point of calm, and so was able to calm him as well.

As she built rapport, Tuff made a series of small, concrete suggestions, some of which he would want to do anyway. She suggested that he drink some of his water. She suggested he sit down. As he got closer to surrendering, she suggested that he unload his pockets. When that went well, she suggested that he put down the gun and put his ammunition on the counter. When he did that, she suggested that he lie down on the floor, and let her help him surrender.

The series of small suggestions works this way: First you get him to do to a small thing he would want to do anyway: sit down, have a drink of water, anything to slow him down. Then you make a further suggestion: respond to you, or tell you his name.

Each small agreement made it a little more likely that Hill would comply again, until Tuff was able to help him peacefully surrender. Meanwhile, she was careful not to overreach, while reassuring Hill he was safe, that it all could end peacefully.

As Hill complied with the surrender, Tuff said she was proud of him, that he was doing a brave thing. This tends to be surprising and quite effective. It's also true—standing down at a moment like that requires far more courage than shooting someone.

Meanwhile, the rest of the school executed their safety protocols, locked the doors, and when signaled, evacuated the students.

Tuff also left her phone connected to 911, so authorities could monitor what was going on. This helped the police make an informed decision about whether or not to storm the building. Be realistic: It's nerve-wracking to wait outside, with no way of knowing where things stand. Under those conditions, even the best professionals can make a mistake. So be wise and help authorities know what's going on, so they can make good decisions.

If a phone is not available, another way to help the police monitor the situation is to quietly flip the one-way switch on an intercom. That way, someone in another room can listen in, and put a phone next to the speaker so the police can stay informed.

Now, some people have argued that because Hill did not enter shooting that this somehow discounts this event. On the contrary: Newtown-style shootings are rare. You are more likely to encounter the student or parent who turns up with a shotgun or butcher knife, angry, agitated, and possibly off their meds.

Tuff provides an exemplary example of how to de-escalate an armed intruder when there's a chance to talk. Next we'll look at what to do when there is no time to talk.

Live Fire

In the past, police advice during a shooting might have been to stay down and wait until the professionals arrive. Police or a SWAT team would be there quickly. Shootings are so fraught with danger, it was thought best to leave action to the pros.

That thinking has since changed. Mass shootings with automatic weapons are nihilistic, causing extensive loss of life in just the few minutes it takes for police to arrive. SWAT teams are highly skilled, but there simply isn't time to wait for their arrival. Instead, it's now thought that laypeople—we teachers, administrators, and even by-standers—are better off taking action.

Police response time has been outstanding. With the prevalence of cell phones, incidents are reported nearly instantly, and police arrive within minutes. Once the police arrive, the pattern has been for the shooter to abruptly change. His actions shift from firing at kids to fighting the police or shooting himself. His focus is no longer on attacking kids.

As a teacher, your role is to get your students through the brief period of time before the police arrive. This may seem to take forever, but again, police response time is usually very fast.

Protecting Students

Any way out is good. Hide. If it's safe to do so, put children out the window. One thing we've learned is that a single person who grasps the situation and takes action quickly can save lives. In one college shooting, lives were saved by a professor who had survived the Holocaust. He recognized gunfire, barricaded the door, and ordered his students out a window. He gave his life holding the door, but many young people were saved.

If there isn't a safe room, get the children out of sight: in a storeroom, a closet, a bathroom, or anyplace where they won't be seen. Examining these incidents, gunmen seem to have the same trouble with clear focus that others have while flooding. One classroom was spared at Newtown because a piece of cardboard was covering the window and had never been removed. The gunman walked past the classroom and never looked in.

Come to know your school layout. If you are substituting in an unfamiliar school, take a few minutes to become familiar with the building. Consider the places to go. Your school should have protocols—if it doesn't, work with administration to develop them. You want to know what to do ahead of time. Regular classroom teachers should have a section at the front of their daybook clearly labeled "emergency procedures." Make large, bright-colored posters and post them at each classroom exit.

Charging a Shooter

Teachers have done astonishingly heroic things in rushing gunmen. While it's an incredible testament to the courage of staff, charging live fire has not been particularly effective. While extraordinarily brave, there's little to show that it especially works.

Instead, the people who successfully intervened made their move as the gunman reloaded or when the gun jammed. After all, a gun is a machine, and machines malfunction. Rushing someone with a gun is still extremely dangerous; there's no way to recommend it. But if you're determined to do it anyway, your best opportunity is if the gun jams or the shooter fumbles while reloading.

If you rush the gunman, you are now in a wrestling match with someone who is probably not in his right mind. Everything's a blur, you can't see what's going on, and there's no time to get your bearings.

Do not look in the gunman's face. You won't like what you see and the information will not help you. It will be hard to see in the confusion, so focus on one thing: where the gun meets the fingers. Twist the gun away or twist back the fingers.

If you break a few of the gunman's fingers in the process, he may not be able to reload or fire. He may not feel the pain because he's flooded with adrenaline, but fingers stop working when broken.

Now, this may sound obvious, but if you get the gun away, never give it back and never let go of the gunman's hands. The norm is for gunmen to have multiple weapons and a great deal of ammunition somewhere about their bodies.

Laurie Dann, who killed one child and injured five others in a school shooting in Winnetka, Illinois, ended up at a nearby house and took the family hostage. She had two guns. The son of the house, home from college, took one of the guns, unloaded it, and returned it to her as a good-faith gesture. When police arrived, she shot him in the chest and then killed herself. He survived to teach crisis negotiation with the FBI.

It's worth noting that Dann, like the Newtown shooter, also lived with her parents, had a known history of mental problems, and was still allowed access to guns. This was another case where an alert family could have saved lives.

Disrupt the Plan

In Florida, there was a case in which a college student who had been recently thrown out of school laid a meticulous plan for a mass shooting at his dorm. Having begun to execute his plan, he turned to shoot his roommate, who had no idea about the gunman's intentions.

The roommate ducked and locked himself in the bathroom. The gunman panicked and shot himself. None of the other planned shootings took place.

Here we have curious behavior. The gunman had already set off fire alarms to bring the police. He was prepared for mayhem and a firefight. But he was not prepared for a change in plan. When things went off-plan, he shot himself.

Often mass shooters plan to shoot themselves at some point. But in the Florida case a relatively simple disruption meant the gunman shot himself before harming anyone else.

As I dealt with people who planned violence, I learned something interesting: They needed to be in control. They often had some fantasy in mind, some magnificent story they wished to live out. Mass shooters take this even further: They develop intricate plans in detail, leading to their personal, glorious Armageddon.

This was their big moment, what they'd planned for and pictured: it *couldn't* go wrong. They didn't deal well with surprises.

In multiple cases with mass shooters, just as things stopped going their way, they shot themselves. It was already part of their plan; it just came sooner or later depending on circumstances.

Prevention Guidelines

With school shootings we can see many of the themes from this book coming back into play.

The best time to stop aggression and violence is before it starts. This was never more true than with mass shootings. Prevention is by far the best solution.

There may be a broad window of opportunity. In all these cases there was a significant period of time, sometimes years, as the situation built. To compare shootings to the Our Lady of Angels' fire, it's the smoldering trash barrel that no one noticed.

Once the crisis explodes, there's no safe way to stop it. But in many cases there has been a window of opportunity. The problem was that, too often, it passed unseen.

You can't change what you can't see. In order to make use of the window of opportunity, you have to notice it's there. In retrospect, some of the clues pointing to mass murder are achingly obvious. People failed to act, not because they're unintelligent, but because they didn't know what to look for.

Once you know what you see, you have to know what to do. Even some people who recognized early that something was terribly amiss didn't carry through with meaningful action. If the next step was unclear, they sometimes failed to act.

Two weeks before the shootings at Newtown, Nancy Lanza, the shooter's mother, e-mailed a friend about being in her son's room and finding horrifying sketches of people being shot. Lanza's mother was deeply disturbed, but wanted to think it over. There is no indication she took basic precautions, like moving the guns or changing the lock on the gun safe.

Nearly all of the people we discussed earlier were puzzled or taken aback by the prospect of murder. It's normal to be baffled by something so unthinkable. But the professor who had survived the Holocaust was not baffled. Because he quickly grasped the nature of the danger, he acted effectively and saved lives.

Normal calm has survival value. Think of the teen who reported the friendly/vicious bomber. He had to feel it through: He didn't feel safe, and something was clearly not right. Kids subjected to everyday chaos have trouble making that distinction. Commonplace threats start to blur together; violence becomes background noise. The de-sensitization to violence has a real survival cost.

Passing the baton is the point where mistakes happen. A student's serious behavioral issues need follow-up as he moves from one school, class-room, or grade to another. Parents need to be actively, competently involved. You can't take this competence for granted.

Support for families is crucial. With mental health concerns, families often become isolated and make poor decisions. They also end up paying the cost. This is a common pattern; blame doesn't change the results. Help families get the help they need.

Bring in skilled professionals early. Prior to a full-blown crisis, trained professionals can do a lot, and do it safely. It's better to bring them in early than to bring them in too late.

Chapter Ten
Newtown and Beyond: Tip Sheet

Prevention is the best approach to school shootings.

We can solve our national problems. However, we have to avoid endless, vituperative blame. Though it may feel emotionally right, it tends to backfire. It doesn't deliver results.

We do not have a single perfect answer to stopping school fires. Instead we have many good answers that, together, save lives.

There is often a window of opportunity to prevent mass attacks. The problem is that it may pass unseen.

Notice and report obsessive interest in automatic weapons or explosives.

Report violent mixed messages. Enthusiasm for mass murder or shooting students isn't friendly chitchat.

A potentially violent kid's computer may be his silent partner. The computer will know what his parents never suspected. Appropriate software could save lives.

If you see something, say something. You have to be alert in order to see something.

Follow up if someone has a history of violence. The same mental health issues may re-emerge years later, especially if something disrupts his or her life: flunking out of school, a divorce in the family, or some other major loss.

Safety Measures

Police in substations in schools are not armed guards. They come and go on an unpredictable schedule, which makes a school a less desirable target.

Safe rooms have been highly effective. Know where yours are, and know how to access them quickly.

Know your plan. Know your building. Your school should have a safety protocol. Know what it is, and know what's expected of you.

De-escalating Someone Armed

Stay calm. If you're scared, don't show it.

Comply with non-violent orders, like calling family or the media. If it's harmless, go ahead and do it.

Talk about yourself as a three-dimensional human being. You'll be less likely to be shot.

Make a series of small suggestions. Start with something the gunman would want to do anyway, like have some water. Each suggestion makes it more likely he will accept the next suggestion. Watch your timing and don't push.

Tell the gunman he still has a future. Tell him he's brave for giving up.

During a Shooting

Get the children out of sight. Stay out of sight until police signal it's safe to move.

If you decide to rush a shooter, wait until he or she pauses to reload or the gun jams. Break fingers; get rid of the gun. Know there is no safe way to do this.

Hold onto the shooter's hands until help arrives. Shooters often have other guns or ammunition hidden about their bodies. Never give a gun back to a shooter.

Disrupt the plan. Delaying tactics or surprises can save lives.

Additional Guidelines for Prevention

Support for families is crucial. Families can be in a position to stop or minimize these attacks, but they need support and practical guidance.

It's normal to be puzzled by murderous behavior, such as happy fantasies of mass killings. Remove the means of attack, or contact professionals and let them do it.

Bring in skilled professionals early. Before a crisis erupts, there's a lot that can be done safely by properly trained professionals.

Postscript: Moving Forward

Caring teachers are the heart of a school. At times, we are the first responders to school violence. But more often, we are witness to the early seeds of violence, as troubling behaviors repeat and intensify. We come to know a lot about our kids. We develop a certain feel for when a kid is just going through a stage and when, perhaps, something more is happening.

As teachers, we not only have the opportunity to see a child's behavior day to day, we also have the opportunity to respond and intervene. And when we respond well and find a way to get through to kids, we can make a critical difference in their lives.

This book was created to bring Virtual Tranquilizer skills to teachers, and give teachers practical ways to head off aggression, in the interest of safety and better learning for everyone. We need to work smarter, not just harder. That means choosing our moment, intervening early rather than late, and choosing our response skillfully, rather than reacting hastily.

In the appendix you'll find a wealth of age-specific resources suggested by teachers in the field. Need the link for animated apps to get kids to stop fighting? Two excellent programs are listed. Want to bring Crisis Intervention Team training to your community? There's a link to a step-by-step guide on how to make that happen.

This book is just a starting point; a desk reference, of course, something to grab in time of need, but also a way to start a conversation. We can find better ways to reach kids. Have that conversation in your school. You do not want to be the only one in your school with de-escalation skills. You want all the teachers practicing these methods, because you want *all* the kids to be calm and safe. If kids come to your class calmer and with better self-regulation, your job will be easier. You'll be less bogged down with discipline, so you can get on with the real work of teaching.

All of us—teachers, parents, administrators, neighbors, and community leaders—have an interest in helping kids grow up safe and healthy so they can become safe, healthy members of the community. When we prevent aggression and violence, we help make that healthy future happen.

Teachers are in the business of building the future. So let's build a safer future for everyone.

Aggression and Violence Prevention Resources for Teachers

As I talked to teachers while researching this book, they had rave reviews for many different books and programs, too many to include in one book. I have included those that seem most relevant and useful, and I have organized the lists by chapter to help you find resources that suit your needs.

Keep in mind, aggression and violence prevention is not one-size-fits-all. Look for the ideas and information that best suit your kids and your classroom.

Some of these resources are provided for parents. You might have opportunities to recommend these resources to parents directly or to groups. Perhaps most important, when you go to parents with a problem, these resources will let you offer a solution as well.

Chapter 5: Grades K–2: The Safe Foundation

For Teachers

Hollenbeck, Kathleen M. *Conflict Resolution Activities That Work! Dozens of Easy and Effective Reading, Writing and Role-Playing Activities That Give Kids the Skills They Need to Get along with One Another.* New York: Scholastic, 2001.

Jones, Tricia S. *Kids Working It Out: Stories and Strategies for Making Peace in Our Schools.* San Francisco: Wiley, John & Sons, 2003.

Kreidler, William J., et al. *Adventures in Peacemaking: A Conflict Resolution Guide for School-Age Programs.* San Diego: Project Adventure, 1996.

Kreidler, William J. *Teaching Conflict Resolution Through Children's Literature: Motivate Students to Get off the Conflict Escalator by Talking Things Through.* San Diego: Project Adventure, 1996.

Levin, Diane E. *Teaching Young Children in Violent Times: Building a Peaceable Classroom.* Washington, DC: National Society for the Education of Young Children, 1994.

Teolis, Beth. *Ready-to-Use Conflict Resolution Activities: Over 100 Step-by Step Lessons with Illustrated Activities -Grades K-6.* San Francisco: John Wiley & Sons, 2002.

Wheeler, Edyth J. *Conflict Resolution in Early Childhood: Helping Children Understand, Manage, and Resolve Conflicts.* Ontario: Pearson Canada, 2003.

Wong, Harry & Rosemary. *The First Days of School: How to Be an Effective Teacher.* Mountain View, CA: Harry K. Wong, 2009.

> Excellent guidelines and tips for establishing basic order and a secure framework for kids.

For Parents

Baker, Jed. *No More Meltdowns: Positive Strategies for Dealing with and Preventing Out-Of-Control Behavior.* Arlington, TX: Future Horizons, 2008.

Chansky, Tamar. *Freeing Your Child from Anxiety: Powerful, Practical Solutions to Overcome Your Child's Fears, Worries, and Phobias.* New York: Crown Publishing Group, 2004.

Rath, Tom. *How Full Is Your Bucket?* Omaha, NE: Gallup Press, 2009.

For Kids
McCloud, Carol. *Have You Filled a Bucket Today? A Guide to Daily Happiness for Kids.* Osprey, FL: Nelson Publishing, 2006.

Munson, Derek. *Enemy Pie.* San Francisco: Chronicle Books, 2000.

A young boy learns that making friends with a boy he dislikes is an effective way to resolve their differences.

O'Neill, Alexis. *The Recess Queen.* New York: Scholastic, 2002.

A student new to the school helps the recess bully make friends.

Woodson, Jacqueline. *Each Kindness.* New York: Penguin Group, 2012.

For Teachers, Parents, and Kids
Buron, Kari D. *When My Worries Get Too Big: A Relaxation Book for Children Who Live with Anxiety.* Shawnee Mission, KS: Autism Asperger Publishing Company, 2006.

This book is helpful for teaching self-calming and focusing strategies for all young children.

Penn, Audrey. *The Kissing Hand.* Terra Haute, IN: Tanglewood Press, 1993.

This much-loved book reassures children who are going to school for the first time.

Chapter 6: Grades 3–6: Insights and Intervention
For Teachers
Drew, Naomi. *No Kidding About Bullying: 125 Ready-to-Use Activities to Help Kids Manage Anger, Resolve Conflicts, Build Empathy, and Get Along.* Minneapolis, MN: Free Spirit Publishing, 2010.

Kreidler, William J. *Conflict Resolution in the Middle School.* Cambridge, MA: Educators for Social Responsibility, 1997.

Toontastic. http://launchpadtoys.com/toontastic/

This free cartoon app for the iPad was developed for kids six and older. While the basic app is free and entirely functional, for a small fee you can access more characters, sound effects, and music. The application received a 5-star rating from CommonSenseMedia.com. An educational review of toontastic is online at http://www.commonsensemedia.org/mobile-app-reviews/toontastic.

For Parents
Glasser, Howard, and Jennifer Easley. *Transforming the Difficult Child: The Nurtured Heart Approach.* Tucson, AZ: Nurtured Heart Publications, 2008.

Highly recommended by parents of challenging children, this book focuses on rewarding positive behavior and increasing children's opportunities to be successful.

For Parents, Teachers, and Kids
Huebner, Dawn. *What to Do When Your Temper Flares: A Kid's Guide to Overcoming Problems with Anger.* Washington, DC: Magination Press, 2007.

This book teaches kids how to cool angry thoughts and control angry actions. It was written by a child psychologist skilled in cognitive behavioral techniques and is most effective when read with an adult.

Verdick, Elizabeth. *How to Take the Grrrr Out of Anger.* Minneapolis, MN: Free Spirit Publishing, 2002.

This book is kid-friendly and accessible. It uses jokes and cartoons to teach students effective strategies to deal with anger without violence.

Chapter 6: Middle School: Fighting

For Parents and Teachers

Simmons, Rachel. *Odd Girl Out: The Hidden Culture of Aggression in Girls*. New York: Mariner Books, 2011.

This *New York Times* bestseller features effective strategies that address bullying and empower girls.

For Parents, Teachers, and Kids

Preller, James. *Bystander*. Harrisonburg, VA: R.R. Donnelley & Sons, 2011.

This is a terrific novel about a seventh-grade student encountering a charismatic and powerful bully. It is a great read-aloud to spark discussion and journaling about bullying.

Go!Animate. http://goanimate.com/

This cartoon app for older children uses cartoon versions of teens and adults. It can be used locally on a PC or by posting cartoons to a private channel on the Web. GoAnimate4Schools.com is an educational version of the app that is available at educational rates. Although the product received only a 3-star rating from Commonsensemedia, it won rave reports from teachers who use cartoons to get small children to stop fighting. An online review can be found here: http://www.commonsensemedia.org/website-reviews/goanimate.

Chapter 7: Parents

For Teachers

How to Make Parents Feel Comfortable During a Parent or Teacher Conference. Retrieved from: http://www.wikihow.com/Make-Parents-Feel-Comfortable-During-a-Parent-or-Teacher-Conference

Teaching Heart. http://www.teachingheart.net/parentteacherconference.html

This site provides a great step-by-step guide to the teacher conference and includes links to many downloadable forms that will help you stay organized.

Thompson, Julia G. *The First-Year Teacher's Survival Guide: Ready-to-Use Strategies, Tools & Activities for Meeting the Challenges of Each School Day*. San Francisco: Jossey Bass, 2013.

This is an excellent reference for both beginning and experienced teachers. Topics covered include (but are not limited to) the following: working well with parents, the importance of regular and effective communication with parents, behaving professionally with parents and colleagues, classroom management, and helping students learn effectively.

Tingley, Suzanne Capek. *How to Handle Difficult Parents: A Teacher's Survival Guide*. Fort Collins, CO: Cottonwood Press, 2006.

This book is a humorous but effective guide to deal with and defuse difficult parents, including helicopter parents.

Whitaker, Todd, and Douglas Fiore. *Dealing with Difficult Parents and with Parents in Difficult Situations*. Larchmont, NY: Eye on Education, 2001.

Chapter 9: Mental Health: Getting Outside Help

For Parents

Hirsch, Glenn S., M.D. "Choosing a Mental Health Professional for Your Child: Who, What, When, Where, Why, and How." New York Child Study Center. 2010. Retrieved from: http://www.aboutourkids.org/families/seeking_professional_help/choosing_mental_health_professional

This is an excellent short article on how to choose a mental health professional to help your child.

For Family and Friends

Amador, Xavier. *I Am Not Sick, I Don't Need Help! How to Help Someone with Mental Illness Accept Treatment.* Peconic, NY: Vida Press, 2011.

This book is an invaluable resource for families of individuals who deny they are mentally ill. Dr. Amador also has a website with free resources and information based on his Listen-Empathize-Agree-Partner strategy. http://www.leapinstitute.org/

How to Start a Crisis Intervention Team Program in Your Community. http://cit.memphis.edu/stepsnew2.php

The column on the left will take you through a step-by-step plan to bringing CIT to your area.

Johnson, Julie Tallard. *Hidden Victims Hidden Healers: An Eight-Stage Healing Process for Families and Friends Of The Mentally Ill.* Edina, MN: PEMA Publications, 2007.

Marsh, Diane T. and Rex M. Dickens. *How to Cope with Mental Illness in Your Family.* Los Angeles: Tarcher, 1998.

Woolis, Rebecca. *When Someone You Love Has a Mental Illness: A Handbook for Family, Friends and Caregivers.* Berkeley, CA: Penguin 1992.

Chapter 10: Mass Shootings: Newtown and Beyond

For Teachers and Parents

Children's National Medical Center. Helping Children Cope After a School Shooting. http://www.childrensnational.org/files/pdf/departmentsandprograms/ichoc/school-shooting.pdf

This is an excellent one-page fact sheet on how to help children cope after a school shooting.

For Kids

Patel, Andrea. *On That Day: A Book of Hope for Children.* Berkeley, CA: Tricycle Press, 2002.

Written after 9/11, this picture book comforts children and reassures them the world is still a hopeful place.

Rogers, Fred. Tragic Events in the News. http://www.fci.org/new-site/par-tragic-events.html

Mr. Rogers' website has a good tip sheet on how parents of younger children can comfort them after a tragic event.

Rylant, Cynthia. *The Stars Will Still Shine.* New York: Harper Collins, 2005.

A litany of experiences that make the world a wonderful place.

Schwiebert, Pat. *Tear Soup: A Recipe for Healing After Loss.* Portland, OR: Grief Watch, 2005.

This book provides comfort for children (8 years and up) as well as adults.